The History of Flight

Intermediate to Advanced ESL Lesson plans

20 ESL Lesson Plans for Intermediate to Advanced Students

Includes:

- Full downloadable Audio
- Student Worksheets
- Teacher Guide

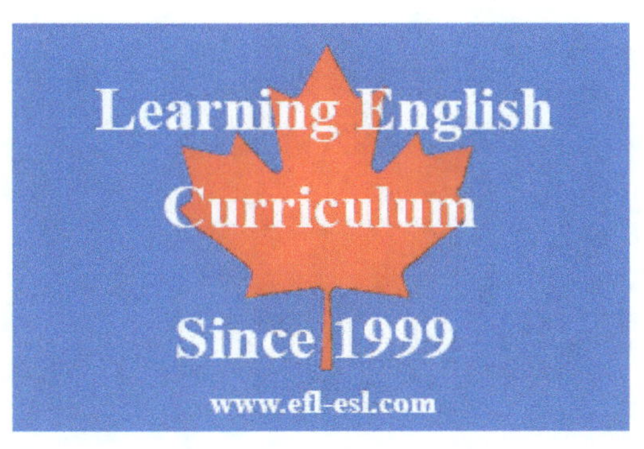

Includes Full Audio

Learning English Curriculum

Published by:
Learning English Curriculum

ISBN 9781772454130

Visit us on the Web at
https://www.efl-esl.com

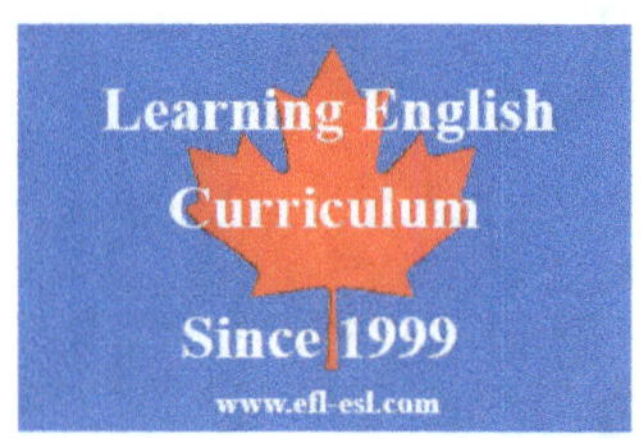

Learning English Curriculum
Victoria, B.C. Canada
E-mail: **info@efl-esl.com**

TEACHING PHILOSOPHY

Our teaching philosophy means that the students and teachers can combine fun and learning, while communicating in English. This is a structured approach, meaning that each new concept is mastered in a conversational English environment before another is introduced. During the past decade, research has shown that the students learn more effectively if the teaching of grammar is integrated with a communicative approach to the learning of the English language.

This program is written for students 13 years and older. We introduce the basic tenses and other structures in a logical sequence, integrating them with light hearted activities that provide practice in a conversational setting. The combination achieved in our curriculum has proved to be popular with the students and successful in achieving its goals.

TIMING AND LESSON STRUCTURE

The most successful order of presentation for the lessons is outlined below:
- Greeting the students in English
- Oral questions (20 to 30 minutes)

Oral Questions may be done before or after the new lesson has been introduced.
The order suggested in the Student's Book should be adapted to the needs of the group.
- Introduction of a new lesson or continuation of a past lesson.
- Completion of exercises and / or partner activities
- Ending with a more relaxed conversational activity

VOCABULARY

The new words introduced in each lesson are listed under the title and may be introduced in any of the following ways:
- The teacher may write the words on the blackboard and use them in sentences.
- The teacher can dramatize, draw or use the pictures to explain the words.
- The students can work in small groups with their dictionaries.

ORAL QUESTIONS

The oral questions are designed to provide practice in speaking.
The questions and answers stress grammatical structure, and word order of the English language.
When our students completed surveys where Oral Questions were rated "helpful / not helpful"
on a scale of 1 to 10, **Oral Questions were consistently rated as "10 - very helpful".**
Teaching this Conversational English program without using the oral questions will result in the lessons becoming too difficult for the students.

These questions provide the basic models of the English Language.
They are a vital part of the program, giving practice, review and an opportunity for the teacher to expand the language to talk about local events.

Contents - Student Reader

Lesson 1   The Dream of Flight   Gerunds   5

Lesson 2   Don't fly too High! Role Play and Questions   7

Lesson 3   Hot Air Balloons   Would Could, Should   10

Lesson 4   Flying Machines   Conditional Sentences   12

Lesson 5 The Zeppelin   Scenarios for Role Play   14

Lesson 6 The Wright Brothers   Debate   16

Lesson 7   Flight in War time   Relationships with Because   19

Lesson 8   The Red Baron Role Play Scenarios, Debate   21

Lesson 9 Rockets and Space Flight   Role play   24

Lesson 10   The Space Race   Passive Voice Role Play Scenarios   26

Lesson 11   Rockets   Debate   29

Lesson 12   The Space Race Cont' Role Play   31

Lesson 13   Moon Landing   Role Play Scenarios   33

Lesson 14   Apollo Missions   Using 'too' Debate   35

Lesson 15   The Hubble Telescope   Role Play   38

Lesson 16 Space Shuttle   Oral Questions   40

Lesson 17   The Canadarm   Oral Questions, Role Play Scenarios   42

Lesson 18   Mars   Oral Questions, Role Play   44

Lesson 19   International Space Station   Role Play Scenarios   48

Lesson 20   Review   50

Final Test (Workbook)   98

Glossary   101

VOCABULARY

fascinate (to)
eagle
kingdom
wing

forth
snake
mythology
throne
righteousness

dragon
heal, to
heel
shine, to
symbol

https://tinyurl.com/2wtn45a9

ACTIVITY 1: Listen to your teacher and or the sound file read the paragraphs, then take turns reading the paragraphs orally.

Have you ever looked at the sky? People are always fascinated with the sky. It changes from minute to minute.

Since very early times, people have watched the birds flying high above their heads. Mythology is full of stories about flying. Mercury was said to be the messenger of the gods. It was said that he had little wings on his hat and heels so he could travel very quickly.

One emperor in Persia was said to have a beautiful throne, and he had eagles that would lift him and his throne high into the sky so that he could see all parts of his kingdom.

Certainly, we know that flight was thought about a lot by people in ancient times. One of the earliest symbols to be found in Egypt is the winged sun. It had an important part in their religion.

Hundreds of years later this symbol was used in the early writings of the Jewish people, and later the same sentence is found in the Bible: "the sun of righteousness will certainly shine forth, with healing in his wings."

Everywhere you look in ancient mythology, you will find creatures that fly. There are flying snakes, flying dragons and all kinds of flying creatures.

The Greeks even had a flying horse called Pegasus.

Pegasus the flying horse

ORAL QUESTIONS TEACHER'S GUIDE

ACTIVITY 2: Divide into small groups. Answer these questions.   Then check your answers.

1. Do you ever wish you could fly like a bird?
2. Who was Mercury?
3. How was Mercury able to move quickly?
4. What was Pegasus?
5. Were flying creatures to be found in ancient mythology?

1. Yes, I sometimes wish I could fly like a bird. No, I don't ever wish I could fly like a bird.
2. Mercury was the messenger of the gods.
3. Mercury had wings on his heels and on his hat.
4. Pegasus was a flying horse.
5. Yes, there were many flying creatures in ancient mythology.

EXERCISE 1 - Workbook page 1
ACTIVITY 3 – Workbook page 1

GERUNDS

A gerund is the – ing form of the verb. It is used as a noun.
It is used in the same way as a noun – as a subject of an object.
Gerunds are used in sentences in three ways:

1. The subject of a sentence:
Flying through the air would be fun.

2. The object of a verb:
I love flying.

3. The object of a preposition:
The birds were tired from flying.

ACTIVITY 3:   Divide into small groups.
Answer these questions using gerunds for the verb given. Then check your answers.

1. Pegasus enjoyed (to fly).

2. Flying can be faster than (to run).

3. Mercury was famous for (to move) quickly.

4. (to fly) creatures were common in mythology.

5. Dragons had wings for (to fly).

6. Early people were fascinated with (to fly).

7. (to fly) is very common today.

8. (to read) about ancient times is interesting.

9. (to find) things to read about in ancient mythology is easy.

10. He always watched the birds (to fly).

1. Pegasus enjoyed flying.

2. Flying can be faster than running.

3. Mercury was famous for moving quickly.

4. Flying creatures were common in mythology.

5. Dragons had wings for flying.

6. Early people were fascinated with flying.

7. Flying is very common today.

8. Reading about ancient times is interesting.

9. Finding things to read about in ancient mythology is easy.

10. He always watched the birds flying.

EXERCISE 2 - Workbook page 2

VOCABULARY

myth	maze	puzzle	garden
bush	design, to	hide, to	prison
escape, to	feather	wax	melt, to
fall apart, to	sea	teach, to	nephew
push, to	tower	partridge	goddess
remember, to			

ACTIVITY 1 : **Listen to the audio and your teacher read the passage, then take turns reading the paragraphs orally.**

Don't try to fly too high!

There is a myth from ancient Greece that talks about flying.

There was a man called Dāedalus who was very smart. The king asked him to make a maze. This is like a giant puzzle, made so that once you are inside, you will never be able to find your way out again. Today, some say that this maze was a huge building with hundreds of halls. However, mostly people believe that it was a huge garden, with rows of bushes, and designed to hide the way out.

After it was finished, the king put Daedalus and his son Ĭcarus in prison. Daedalus watched the birds, and decided that flying would be the only way for them to escape. He made two big wings for himself, using feathers and wax. When he tried the new wings, he found that he could fly like a bird. He made a second pair of wings and gave them to Icarus. He taught Icarus how to fly.

Just before they escaped he told Icarus that he mustn't fly too high. He said that the sun would melt the wax and his wings would fall apart.

Icarus was a young boy, and he loved flying. He didn't listen to his father and flew very high, close to the sun. The sun melted his wings, and Icarus fell into the sea and died.

Later, Daedalus was living in the palace of another king. Because he was very smart, he made many new things. He was asked to teach the king's nephew, Perdix, how to make things. Soon Daedalus found that Perdix was smarter than he was.

One day, Daedalus pushed Perdix off a high tower. Minerva the goddess saw this. She didn't want him to die, so she changed him into a partridge. The partridge flew safely to the ground. Today everyone knows that partridges don't fly into high places and they make their nests on the ground. It is said they still remember, and are afraid to fly too high.

EXERCISE 1: Workbook page 3
ORAL QUESTIONS TEACHER'S GUIDE
 Role-play this conversation with your teacher,

ACTIVITY 2: then role-play it in small groups.

https://tinyurl.com/ympkhdx6

Narrator:	The two friends are talking about Daedalus and Icarus.
Paul:	This story shows that even people a long time ago thought about flying.
Julia:	Well, it was a great way to get away from the king!
Paul:	It wasn't so great for Icarus. He fell into the sea!
Julia:	That was because he didn't listen to his father.
Paul:	Young boys don't like to listen to their fathers.
Julia:	Maybe that's why the story is remembered. It was meant to teach a lesson.
Paul:	I think you're right, Julia.

EXERCISE 2: Workbook page 3
EXERCISE 3: Workbook page 4

ACTIVITY 2 :   **Divide into small groups.
Ask each other the questions, then check your answers.**

1. What did Mercury do?

2. How did the Persian emperor see his kingdom?

3. Were there flying creatures in ancient mythology?

4. What was the name of the flying horse?

5. Do you think flying would be fun?

6. Were early people fascinated with flying?

7. Why did Daedalus make wings?

8. What were the wings made of?

9. What happened to Icarus?

10. Who was Perdix?

11. Why didn't Daedalus like Perdix?

12. What did Daedalus do to Perdix?

13. Who saved Perdix?

1. Mercury was the messenger of the gods.

2. He had eagles lift him and his throne into the air.

3. Yes, there were many flying creatures in ancient mythology.

4. Pegasus was the flying horse's name.

5. Yes, I think flying would be fun. No, I don't think flying would be fun.

6. Yes, early people were fascinated with flying.

7. He wanted to escape from prison.

8. The wings were made of feathers and wax.

9. He fell into the sea and died.

10. Perdix was the king's nephew.

11. He didn't like Perdix because Perdix was smarter than he was.

12. Daedalus pushed Perdix off a high tower.

13. The goddess Minerva saved Perdix.

taffeta	contraption	experiment	lift, to
upwards	cordage	astonishing	rope
balloon	demonstration	land, to	contain, to
destroy, to	untrue		

ACTIVITY 1: **Listen to the audio and your teacher read the paragraphs, then take turns reading out loud.**

In 1777, a French papermaker by the name of Joseph Montgolfier was watching clothes dry over a fire. He noticed that sometimes the wet clothes were lifted up by the hot air. He wanted to find out why this happened so he started doing experiments with hot air. He believed that the smoke contained a gas, which he called "Montgolfier Gas," which could lift things.

He made a box of very thin wood, and covered it with taffeta, and set it on a table with a hole in the middle. He lit a fire under the table. The smoke went upwards through the hole, and lifted the box right off the table. Joseph became very excited and asked his brother Jacques-Étienne to come and see his experiment. He said:
"Get in a supply of taffeta and of cordage, quickly, and you will see one of the most astonishing sights in the world."

They built a much bigger contraption out of thin wood and taffeta and built a fire under it. Suddenly, it took off. Both of them held the ropes, but it pulled upwards so hard they couldn't hold it. Up, up it went, high over the buildings of Paris. Finally, the fire died down and it fell to the street. People who saw this strange, smoky thing fall on their street ran out and destroyed it. They didn't know that this was the first successful flight of a hot air balloon. That was the 14th of December, 1782.

The Montgolfier brothers could see that this experiment could be a real success, so they worked hard on a new design. At first they thought that it might not be safe for people to fly in their balloon, so they sent a sheep, a duck and a rooster on the next flight.

A huge crowd came to see the demonstration, including King Louis XVI and Marie Antoinette. The flight was very successful. The balloon went up about 500 meters and traveled about 3 kilometers.

Although the flight was a great success, and the sheep, duck and rooster landed safely, King Louis was not very happy with the demonstration. The Montgolfier brothers believed that the smoke contained the "Montgolfier Gas" so they made the fire very smoky. They threw in lots of grass and some old boots to make a lot of smoke. All of this smoke looked wonderful to the crowd, but it blew in the face of the king, and he didn't like it!

CONDITIONAL SENTENCES

There are three words that are used for conditional sentences:

COULD – to be able   **WOULD -** expresses intention   **SHOULD** - duty

Conditional sentences use **could** to **express doubt**,
so they are often preceded or followed by an "if" clause:

If I got home early I **could** help my mother.

Would is used to **ask politely** for something:
I **would** like coffee, please.

Should is used to **express a duty** to do something:
We **should** visit my aunt in the hospital.

CONDITIONAL SENTENCES: UNTRUE FACTS IN THE PRESENT TENSE
CLAUSE: A clause is a group of words that has a subject and a verb.

Clause 1   **Clause 2**
I would meet her at 7:00   if she weren't at work.

If the sentence **is untrue at the time**, use the **past tense** in the "if" clause.
"Were" is used for both singular and plural in conditional sentences.
If I were rich, I would buy a new car
If I were a dog, I would chase cats.

ACTIVITY 2:   **Divide into small groups. Ask each other the questions,**
then check your answers.

1. If you were there, would you fly in their balloon?

2. Would the king have liked it if there were no smoke?

3. If you could, would you fly in a balloon?

4. If you had time would you make a balloon?

5. If you had some "Montgolfier Gas", could it lift you up?

6. If you were a rooster would you like a balloon ride?

7. If you were Joseph Montgolfier would you be happy?

---

1. Yes, if I were there I would fly in their balloon.
   No, if I were there I wouldn't fly in their balloon.
2. Yes, he would have liked it if there were no smoke.
3. Yes, if I could I would fly in a balloon. No, if I could I wouldn't fly in a balloon.
4. Yes, if I had time I would make a balloon. No, if I had time I wouldn't make a balloon.
5. If I had some "Montgolfier Gas" it wouldn't lift me.
   There isn't a gas called "Montgolfier Gas".
6. No, if I were a rooster I wouldn't like a balloon ride.
7. Yes, if I were Joseph Montgolfier I'd be happy.

VOCABULARY

kite	religious	ceremony	platform
handle	pilot	attempt, to	record, to
glider	balloon	electric	motor
helicopter	model	repair, to	hydrogen

ACTIVITY 1: **Listen to the audio and your teacher read the paragraphs, then take turns reading orally.**

About 2,000 years ago the Chinese people became very good at making kites. At first they were used for religious ceremonies, then later, they flew them just for fun.

In the fifteenth century, Leonardo da Vinci made a beautiful drawing of a flying machine, that was like a helicopter. In his drawing, the pilot stood on a platform and turned a handle very quickly. This turned wings above the pilot's head and made the machine rise into the air.

People have made machines like the da Vinci drawing, but they can't make them fly. The machines were too heavy. Maybe it was just his dream.

After that, we have no records of any attempts to fly until 1799. An Englishman, Sir George Caley designed the first small model airplane. In 1804 he flew the model with a small engine. At that time, engines powerful enough to do the work were too heavy for big planes to lift.

A German, Otto Lilienthal did a lot of work with gliders. He was very interested in the flight of birds, and thought that if we had wings like birds, we could fly. In many ways, he was like a modern scientist, because he made a record of all his flights.
In fact, his records helped all of the later experimenters in flight.

Otto Lilienthal made more than 2500 flights in the gliders he made. Very little was known about flying then, and so it was dangerous work. There were many crashes, and Lilienthal had to repair his gliders many times. Unfortunately, he was killed in a crash in 1896.

While Lilienthal was working on his gliders, other people were working with balloons. With hot air or hydrogen, balloons could be lighter than air, while planes were always heavier than air. Finally, in 1884, a big balloon called La France flew around the Eiffel Tower in Paris. It had a small electric motor. It flew 8 kilometers in 23 minutes.

Because it was controlled by a motor, this is said to be the first flight made by man.

ORAL QUESTIONS TEACHER'S GUIDE

ACTIVITY 2: Workbook page 8

ACTIVITY 3:   **Divide into small groups. Ask each other the questions, then check your answers.**

1. Did the Chinese people make airplanes?	1. No, they made kites.
2. Did they fly in their kites?	2. No, they didn't fly in their kites.
3. Did Leonardo da Vinci's flying machine fly?	3. No, his machine didn't fly.
4. Where was Otto from?	4. Otto was from Germany.
5. Did he have motors in his flying machines?	5. No, he didn't have motors.
6. Did he make many glider flights?	6. Yes, he made many glider flights.
7. How did he help other people interested in flying?	7. He made a record of all his flights.
8. What happened to Otto ?	8. He died when his glider crashed.
9. What were people using to lift their balloons?	9. People were using hot air and hydrogen to lift their balloons.
10. Were the balloons heavier than air?	10. No, the balloons were lighter than air.
11. Were the gliders heavier than air?	11. Yes, the gliders were heavier than air.
12. What was the name of the first balloon that flew around the Eiffel Tower?	12. The first balloon that flew around the Eiffel Tower was called La France.

USING CONDITIONAL SENTENCES IN THE FUTURE TENSE

If the future tense **"will"** is used, put the **"if clause"** or **the conditional clause,** into the **present tense.**

EXAMPLES:
I will tell him if I **see** him.
He will understand if I **tell** him.
I'll buy a car when I **get** there.

ACTIVITY 4:   **Divide into small groups. Complete the sentences, then check your answers.**

1. I will see you when I (to get)__________there.	1. I will see you when I get there.
2. I will cook some apples if I (to have) __________them.	2. I will cook some apples if I have them.
3. The children will run if they (to see) __________me.	3. The children will run if they see me.
4. You will get sick if you (to sleep, not) __________.	4. You will get sick if you don't sleep.
5. You will be late if you (to hurry, not) __________.	5. You will be late if you don't hurry.
6. I will be glad if they (to give) __________me supper.	6. I will be glad if they give me supper.
7. I won't be able to give you any if I (to have, not) __________ any.	7. I won't be able to give you any if I don't have any.
8. I will eat supper if there (to be) __________any.	8. I will eat supper if there is any.

EXERCISE 1: Workbook page 8

EXERCISE 2: Workbook page 9

VOCABULARY

patent, to
wealthy
accident
transatlantic
scenario

reconnaissance
enemy
airline
engine

destination
Civil War
company
cabin

passenger
engineer
enormous
ocean

ACTIVITY 1: **Listen to the audio and your teacher read the paragraphs, then take turns reading orally.**

THE ZEPPELIN

During the American Civil War, (1861 to 1865), the Union army used balloons to fly up over the enemy lines and see what they were doing. Five years later, the French used balloons in the Franco-Prussian War.

A German, Count von Zeppelin became very interested in balloons. With his friends, he designed a huge balloon. One of the people who worked with him was Gottlieb Daimler, an engineer, who later was active in working with gas engines.

The zeppelins had one or two cabins underneath the balloon for carrying people. The balloon was filled with hydrogen. The first zeppelin flight was in 1900. Count von Zeppelin patented his design in 1895.

At first there were a lot of terrible crashes. By 1908, however, their experiments were becoming very successful. In that year Count von Zeppelin formed the first airline company in the world.

Zeppelins were used a lot in the First World War. The Germans used them for reconnaissance, and some even dropped bombs.

In 1929, the "Graf Zeppelin" flew around the world!

Count Zeppelin's company built two huge zeppelins, the "Hindenburg" and the "Graf Zeppelin". These were enormous airships. The "Hindenburg" was of 245 meters long and it could carry 200 tons. After the first war, the airline company set up passenger service. They started transatlantic flights in the 1930's These were the first passengers to ever fly across an ocean.

Many of the wealthy people in the world wanted to fly across the ocean. There were regular flights from Germany to cities in North and South America.

This wonderful period in the history of flight came to a fiery ending in 1937. The Hindenburg exploded and burned while landing in New York.

ORAL QUESTIONS TEACHER'S GUIDE

EXERCISES 1 and 2: Workbook page 10

ACTIVITY 2:   Divide into small groups. Role play the following scenarios:
Write your conversation in a notebook, and be ready to role-play it for the class.

Scenario 1:
You are a group of young people. You have read about the zeppelins, and are talking about the early trans Atlantic flights. One of the group thinks it would be wonderful to float across the ocean in a zeppelin. One of the group thinks that it was just something that the rich people did to show their friends that they had lots of money, and that they weren't afraid. Others in the group had different ideas. Make this into a good conversation.

Scenario 2:
Your group is trying to think what it was like to go on one of the first flights across the ocean. You are talking about how fast it would go to get there in a short time – so much faster than by boat. One of your group is thinking that it would be very scary, but another is saying that it would be quite safe, because the zeppelin is over 240 meters long. Make this into a good conversation.

Scenario 3:
One of your group is saying that he/ she would like to go on a zeppelin across the ocean. It would be exciting. Another person is saying that they wouldn't like to go in a zeppelin because there might be a big wind, and it would blow the zeppelin away. Another person is saying that they think it would be too dangerous, because the zeppelin is filled with hydrogen, and it might explode. Make this into a good conversation.

Scenario 4:
In your group, one person has found that it is possible to have a ride in a hot air balloon. He / she is suggesting that if each person were to pay fifty dollars, they could all go in the balloon for an hour's ride.
One person heard that there were a couple of accidents in the United States in 2007, so they don't think it's safe. Another person likes the idea, and suggests all the things that they would see. Another person hasn't got fifty dollars, and says that even if they did have the money, they wouldn't spend it that way. Make this into a good conversation.

EXERCISE 3: Workbook page 10

VOCABULARY

aviator	automobile	force	upright
reassemble, to	track	accelerate, to	steady, to
concern, to	control, to	wind tunnel	discover, to
own, to	cylinder	propeller	spin, to
journal	reporter	faint	glimpse

ACTIVITY 1: **Listen to the audio and your teacher read the passage, then take turns reading orally.**

https://tinyurl.com/5n84h2uh

In the early 1900's Orville and Wilbur Wright became interested in flight. At first, they thought about building an automobile, but later decided that it wouldn't sell.

The two brothers owned a bicycle shop. They were fascinated by the forces that held the bike upright when it was traveling. Although neither of them finished high school, they were very smart. They spent a lot of time studying books on flight. They were sure that if they could designed their plane right, it would fly steadily in the air, just like a bicycle travels down a road. Because of their ideas about bicycles, Orville and Wilbur were the only early aviators that were concerned about how to control the movements of the airplane. They wanted to be able to control whether it went up or down, turned right or left, or whether it would roll over.

They built a wind tunnel, and tried all different shapes of wings. They made many model planes for their wind tunnel, to try these different shapes. At first all of their models crashed, but they kept trying. Finally, they discovered a good shape for the wings. Then they started making gliders.

The two brothers made over 1,000 flights in their gliders, trying to find the best design.

Wilbur Wright

When they were ready, they started looking for a gas engine for their airplane. At that time, gas engines were very heavy. To make an airplane move along the ground and then take off needs a lot of power. Any gas engine that they could find that was powerful enough, was much too heavy for their airplane. Finally, Wilbur and Orville built their own engine. It weighed just 70 kilograms.

All of the work that they did in designing the right shape for the wings helped them with the propeller design. They found that they could have a propeller spinning around at a great rate, without doing much work. So they designed and made their own propellers.

Orvbille Wright

Finally, they were ready. They sent the pieces of their plane to Kitty Hawk in North Carolina, then went down and reassembled their plane. They chose Kitty Hawk, because they were told that there was always a wind there.

They moved their plane to the top of a hill and set it on a track. Wilbur took the first turn as pilot. The plane accelerated down the track so quickly that Orville, who was running beside it to steady the wing, couldn't keep up. One wing broke when the plane turned and hit the hill.

December 17th 1903, three days later, was to be an historic day. They put the track on some flat ground and used the wind to move the plane along. Orville was the pilot while Wilbur ran beside it to steady the wing. The plane lifted off the ground for 12 seconds and flew for 120 feet. It was one of the great events of the century. He made the first heavier-than-air, machine powered flight in the world! Orville did what men and women had only dreamed of doing for centuries.

They flew three times that day. The last flight took Wilbur 825 feet in 59 seconds. On that day the Wright brothers made history.

ORAL QUESTIONS TEACHER'S GUIDE

ACTIVITY 2: **Divide into small groups. Ask each other the questions, then check your answers.**

1. Why did they build a wind tunnel?	1. They wanted to study how the wind affected their models.
2. Did the Wright brothers fly in gliders?	2. Yes they flew in gliders (many times).
3. What was the problem with the early gas engines?	3. They were too heavy for airplanes.
4. How did they get a gas engine that was light enough?	4. They built their own gas engine.
5. Why did they choose Kitty Hawk to fly their plane?	5. They chose Kitty Hawk because there is usually a wind there.
6. Did their plane fly on the first day in Kitty Hawk?	6. No, it crashed on the first day.
7. Who was the pilot on the first flight?	7. Orville was the pilot on the first flight.
8. Did their plane stay up for long?	8. No, it only stayed up for 12 seconds.
9. How far did their plane go on its first flight?	9. The plane flew 120 feet.
10. How far did Wilbur fly on the last flight that day?	10. On the last flight Wilbur flew 825 feet.

ACTIVITY 3: WORKBOOK PAGE 12
EXERCISES 1 & 2: WORKBOOK PAGE 13
EXERCISES 3: WORKBOOK PAGE 14

ACTIVITY 4:
SEATING

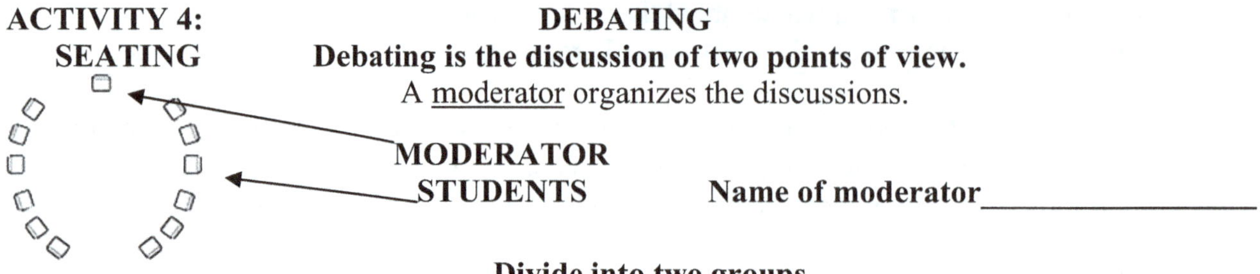

DEBATING
Debating is the discussion of two points of view.
A <u>moderator</u> organizes the discussions.

Name of moderator______________________

Divide into two groups.

Group 1 agrees with the statement.   **Group 2 doesn't agree with the statement.**
We say they are "**Pro**"   We say they are "**Con**".

The statement to be discussed today is: **It isn't necessary to have an education to do well in life.**

The moderator is between the groups but at one end.
The two groups are often referred to as **Pro** and **Con**.
Each group brainstorms and writes down
ideas that support what they think.

One person from each group
will present their group's ideas to the large group.

It is very important that the students
sit with the two groups facing each other.

Return to the large group

Moderator: **The statement for today is: It isn't necessary to have an education to do well in life.**

Moderator: Now we will hear from Group 1, speaking for the Pro side.

Now we will hear from Group 2, speaking for the Con side.

Now <u>everyone</u> in the room, except the Moderator, should say why they agree or disagree with the statement. They are to think of as many things as they can. Unusual or funny ideas are very good. Remember, you are learning English, not solving the problems of the world.

VOCABULARY

unfortunately	invention	weapon	observation
military	aircraft	eventually	battle
prediction	attackers	government	bravery
risky		grenade	hero

ACTIVITY 1:   Listen to the audio and your teacher read the passage, then take turns reading.

Unfortunately, mankind usually turns his best inventions into weapons of war. In 1909, just six years after the first flight, the American government ordered its first military plane from the Wright brothers. It was to be used for observation of the enemy's soldiers.

The plane they built had two seats – one for the pilot and one for an observer. It was able to fly at speeds up to 64 kilometers per hour, and was able to stay in the air for an hour without running out of fuel.

The first military flight was made in 1911, by an Italian, Captain Carlo Piazza. In the Italo-Turkish war, he flew a plane over the Turkish army to see where they were, and how strong they were.

Also in 1911, the first British military officer to fly, Captain Bertram Dickenson, had this to say: "Aircraft would first be used for reconnaissance purposes, and this would eventually turn into a battle to control the skies."

Soon, during the First World War, both sides used Zeppelins to drop bombs on the enemy, and planes were sent up to fight off attackers.

When planes first started to be used in warfare, the pilots didn't quite know what to do about other pilots when they saw them. The planes were open, and it was very easy for the pilots to see each other. So, as the planes passed each other, the pilots would wave. Later, they decide that they should try to stop the enemy pilots, so they started to carry rocks and even grenades in their planes, so they could throw them at the other pilots. Some pilots even carried pieces of rope with them. They threw them at the other aircraft, hoping the rope would get caught in the enemy's propeller, and stop the plane.

Some of the pilots became very good at flying. They also had the soldiers on the ground shooting at them so it was risky. A number of the first pilots became great heroes because of their bravery. It was very dangerous, and quite a few men were killed.

Finally, all of the military aircraft had heavy machine guns, and the day of air wars began. Captain Dickenson was right.

ORAL QUESTIONS TEACHER'S GUIDE

EXERCISES 1 & 2 – WOKKBOOK PAGE 15

SHOWING RELATIONSHIPS

because -   **is used to express expected results**
I eat dinner <u>because</u> I'm hungry.

even though or **although** are used to add an unexpected part (result) to a sentence.
I went to town, <u>even though</u> (although) I didn't want to buy anything.

so -   **is used to show that something is the result of something else**
I finished my work <u>so</u> I went home.

but -   shows unexpected results   **or**   direct opposition
He was sick <u>but</u> he went to work.   She was very poor <u>but</u> he was rich.

but...anyway -   **is used to show unexpected - opposite results.**
It was raining <u>but</u> they had a picnic <u>anyway</u>.

ACTIVITY 2:   Divide into small groups.

Make sentences using <u>because</u>, <u>even though</u>, <u>although</u>, <u>so</u>, <u>but</u>, or <u>but...anyway</u>. Then check for *possible* answers in the box.

1.   they had many failures, Orville and Wilbur kept trying
2.   it was very dangerous, the pilots kept flying
3.   they kept working Orville and Wilbur knew they could do it
4.   zeppelins dropped bombs enemy aircraft shot them down
5.   later they tried to shoot them down at first the pilots waved to each other
6.   the government saw good uses for aircraft in times of war they ordered a warplane
7.   they waved at each other they were enemies
8.   many died there were some very good pilots
9.   neither brother finished high school they were both very smart

1.   Even though / although they had many failures, Orville and Wilbur kept trying.
2.   It was very dangerous, but the pilots kept flying.
3.   Orville and Wilbur knew they could do it so they kept working.
4.   Zeppelins dropped bombs, so enemy aircraft shot them down.
5.   At first the pilots waved to each other, but later they tried to shoot them down.
6.   The government saw good uses for aircraft in times of war so they ordered a warplane
7.   Even though / although they were enemies they waved at each other.
8.   Although / even though there were some very good pilots, many died.
9.   They were both very smart, but neither brother finished high school.

(There may be other ways to make correct sentences using the words given.

Try to find different ways to make good sentences.)
EXERCISES 3 – WOKKBOOK PAGE 16
EXERCISES 4 – WOKKBOOK PAGE 17

VOCABULARY

baron	combat	unit	earn, to	flyer
elite	force	ace	equipment	tent
headquarters	battlefield	tent	triplane	determine, to
rank	accept, to	eventually	chase, to	lucky

https://tinyurl.com/4ma9uzwt

ACTIVITY 1   Listen to the audio and your teacher read the passage, then take turns reading.

One of the most interesting and famous of the early fliers was Captain Manfred Albrecht von Richthofen. Not many people will remember that name, most remember his other name: The Red Baron.

In 1915 he joined the German Flying Service, later to be called the Luftwaffe. In August of 1916 he asked to be transferred to a flying combat unit. He soon earned a reputation for bravery. In November of that year, he shot down Britain's top flyer, Major Lanoe Hawker.

In 1917 he was asked to form a small, elite force of ace fliers. Germany wanted a small force of good fliers who could move quickly to other parts of the battlefield. They had little equipment, so they used large tents for their headquarters. Because these tents were colorful, the group became known as "Richthofen's Flying Circus." They decided to have red on all of their planes so they could be easily seen. Richthofen's plane was all red. This is why he was called "The Red Baron." It meant that the enemy planes could easily see him and would try to shoot him down, but he was very successful.

Richthofen was determined to make his small group of pilots the very best. He made a list of rules for all the pilots in his group, and this certainly saved many of their lives. It was a very dangerous job. Enemy planes could find them and shoot them down, or their own plane might give problems and crash. The planes of the day were very fragile. Richthofen flew in a triplane for a while in 1917. A triplane has three sets of wings.

Because he was so successful, he should have had the rank of Major, or Lieutenant Colonel. However, in the German Military at that time, he couldn't accept a rank higher than his father, so the Red Baron remained a Captain. The Red Baron shot down 80 enemy planes, which is more than any other pilot in the First World War. He was eventually wounded in the head in July 1917. This kept him from flying for some weeks, but then he started flying again.

Early in 1918, Captain Manfred Albrecht von Richthofen, The Red Baron, was finally shot down. He was chasing an enemy plane over enemy lines when he was shot from the ground. Although he was only 26 when he died, he is thought to be one of the greatest fliers ever known.

ORAL QUESTIONS TEACHER'S GUIDE

ACTIVITY 2:

**Divide into small groups. Answer the questions.
Then check the answers in the box.**

1. What was Captain Manfred von Richthofen called?
2. Why was he called that?
3. Was he a good pilot?
4. Why was their group called "The Red Baron's Flying Circus"?
5. Was it a dangerous job?
6. Did the Red Baron shoot down many enemy planes?
7. Why do you think enemy planes could easily see him?
8. What is a triplane?
9. Was the Red Baron ever wounded?
10. How did the Red Baron die?

1. He was called "The Red Baron."
2. He was called that because he flew a red airplane.
3. Yes, he was a very good pilot.
4. They stayed in colorful tents.
5. Yes, it was a very dangerous job.
6. Yes, he shot down 80 enemy planes.
7. They could see him easily because his plane was red.
8. It's a plane with three sets of wings.
9. Yes, he was wounded in the head.
10. He was shot down by the enemy.

EXERCISES 1 & 2 – WORKBOOK PAGE 18

ACTIVITY 3: **Divide into small groups. Role play the following scenarios:**
Write your conversation in a notebook, and be ready to role-play it for the class.

Scenario 1:

One of your group thinks that the Red Baron was a real hero. He flew in an open plane and faced terrible dangers for his country. Others in the group disagree. They think that he was crazy to take such risks. Another person makes an observation about the eighty enemy pilots that he killed during the war. Make a conversation and present it to the class.

Scenario 2:

Your group is talking about flight. They talk about the very small planes that were used in the First World War, and how much air travel has changed since that day. Make a conversation and present it to the class.

Scenario 3:

Your group is talking about all the great men and women who have had wonderful ideas in the past and worked hard, like the Wright Brothers to make their inventions work. Make a conversation and present it to the class.

EXERCISE 3 – WORKBOOK PAGE 19

ACTIVITY 4:
SEATING

DEBATING
Debating is the discussion of two points of view.
A <u>moderator</u> organizes the discussions.

MODERATOR
STUDENTS   Name of moderator_________________

Divide into two groups.

Group 1 agrees with the statement.   **Group 2 doesn't agree with the statement.**
We say they are "**Pro**"   We say they are "**Con**".

The statement to be discussed today is: **Most good inventions are eventually used for warfare.**

The moderator is between the groups but at one end.
The two groups are often referred to as **Pro** and **Con**.
Each group brainstorms and writes down
ideas that support what they think.

One person from each group
will present their group's ideas to the large group.

It is very important that the students
sit with the two groups facing each other.

Return to the large group

Moderator: **The statement for today is: Most good inventions are eventually used for warfare.**

Moderator: Now we will hear from Group 1, speaking for the Pro side.

Now we will hear from Group 2, speaking for the Con side.

Now <u>everyone</u> in the room, except the Moderator, should say why they agree or disagree with the
statement. They are to think of as many things as they can. Unusual or funny ideas are very good.
Remember, you are learning English, not solving the problems of the world.

VOCABULARY

refer, to	anthem	fireworks	improve, to	orbit, to
radio wave	reaction	plan, to	accomplish, to	nuclear bomb
deliver, to	satellite	launch, to	canon ball	canon
develop, to	glare	unable	rocket	

ACTIVITY 1: **Listen to the audio and your teacher read the passage, then take turns reading orally.**

When you see beautiful fireworks in the night sky, you can thank the Chinese people for this. They were the first to use rockets. The rockets were small, containing a small bomb, which they hoped would start a fire. Although we are not certain, it seems that the Chinese were using rockets before the year 1000 AD. We know that the Arabs used rockets against the French in 1248.

The British did a lot of work to improve rockets for use in warfare. In 1806, they completely destroyed the French town of Boulogne when they fired 2000 rockets into the town. Fires from the rockets burned all the buildings, and the French felt unable to fight.

Rockets were used in the war of 1812, and Francis Scott Key referred to "the rockets' red glare" when she wrote the national anthem of the United States.

On October 4th, 1957 the Russians launched Sputnik I, and started a whole new era in human history. Now we call it the "Space Age". This small ball was carried into space by a powerful rocket, and started orbiting the earth. This satellite circled the earth every 98 minutes, and sent back radio waves. The sounds of these radio waves were heard by people all over the world on their radios.

The first reaction was surprise. The Americans were planning on launching a satellite, but Sputnik was many times heavier than what they were planning. No one knew that the Russians would be able to accomplish this.

The next reaction was fear. Everyone knew that the Russians had nuclear bombs. Now, everyone could see that they also had rockets that could deliver a nuclear bomb to any part of the world. Then, just a month later, the Russians launched Sputnik II, a much heavier satellite than the first.

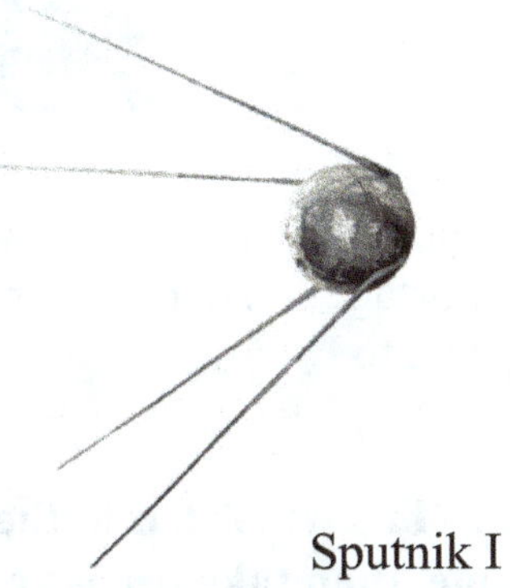

Sputnik I

The Americans formed a new department called the National Aeronautics and Space Administration, or NASA, and did some very good work with rockets to catch up to the Russian space program.

ACTIVITY 2: Divide into groups and role play the dialogue several times.

You: I read that during the American Civil War, the military learned how to make much better cannons, so rockets weren't used.

Friend 1: Why is that?

Friend 2: The cannons could shoot a large cannon ball a long distance. The early rockets couldn't carry anything as heavy, and they couldn't shoot as far.

Friend 1: What about rockets?

You: Everything changed in the Second World War. Hitler developed some heavy rockets, and sent them to bomb England. They were terrible.

Friend 2: Although they weren't very accurate, they killed a lot of people and destroyed many buildings.

Friend 1: What happened after the war?

You: The governments saw that rockets could carry nuclear bombs, so they worked hard to develop good rockets. They told the people they wanted to explore space, but they really wanted to control space, so they could drop bombs wherever they wanted.

ORAL QUESTIONS TEACHER'S GUIDE

EXERCISES 1 AND 2 – WORKBOOK PAGE 20
ACTIVITY 3 – WORKBOOK PAGE 21

success	plan, to	arrange, to	survive, to
postage	stamp	return, to	blast off
die, to	mutt	capsule	history

ACTIVITY 1: Listen to the audio and your teacher read the passage, then take turns reading orally.

After the success of Sputnik I, Nikita Khrushchev, the Soviet leader, wanted a second spacecraft launched on November 7, the 40th anniversary of the Bolshevik Revolution.

This was just under five weeks after the launch of Sputnik I, but what Nikita Krushchev wanted, he got. The Russians scientists had another satellite planned, but it wouldn't be ready in time. They were forced to change their plans, and quickly arrange to launch Sputnik II on November 7th.

The scientists wanted to see if a living creature could survive blast off and live in space. They found a dog on the streets of Moscow. They named it Laika, and this dog became the most famous dog in history. This was the first creature to fly into space!

When the flight was finished, the Russians could not get the capsule back, so Laika died. It was a very famous dog, but it was dead.

In the Western world, a dog is often called a "mutt." Soon the newspapers in the West were calling Laika "Muttnik", because she flew in Sputnik.

Laika, which means "Barker," became famous. Different countries in the Soviet Union made stamps with a picture of this dog.

The Russians used many dogs in their space program, all of them picked up off the streets of Moscow. Life was likely difficult on the streets, but did the dogs enjoy traveling in rockets?

There was one dog, whose name was Bold. The Russian scientists had Bold ready for a dangerous space flight. The night before the flight, Bold disappeared. She ran into the forest around the space center.

The scientists had to send another dog into space instead of Bold. A couple of days later, Bold returned. Maybe she didn't want to fly.

ORAL QUESTIONS TEACHER'S GUIDE

THE PASSIVE
The passive is formed by using the verb "to be" plus the past participle

The passive is most often used when we don't know,
or when it is not important who does the action.

ACTIVE: (regular word order) The Americans sent a satellite into orbit.
PASSIVE: A satellite was sent into orbit.

If it is important to know who does the action, "by" is used.

ACTIVE: (regular word order) Good pilots flew the planes.
PASSIVE: The planes were flown by good pilots.

In the passive form, "to be" can be used in different tenses.
Lots of satellites were sent into orbit around the earth.
Lots of satellites are being sent into orbit around the earth.
Lots of satellites will be sent into orbit around the earth.

ACTIVITY 2:
Divide into groups of two or three.
One person is to read the sentences. The other(s) are to give the passive form.
Check your answers in the box.

1. People saw beautiful fireworks in the night sky.
2. The Chinese people made the first rockets.
3. The Arabs also used rockets
4. The British destroyed the town of Boulogne with rockets.
5. Fires from the rockets burned the buildings.
6. The Germans used rockets in World War 2.
7. The Germans developed heavy rockets.
8. The rockets killed many people.
9. In 1957 the Russians launched Sputnik I.
10. They sent Laika into space.
11. The British improved rockets a lot.
12. Strong rockets carried Sputnik into orbit.
13. Sputnik sent radio sounds back to Earth.
14. A month later the Russians launched Sputnik II.
15. People called Laika Mutnick.
16. Smart scientists developed the rockets.

1. Beautiful fireworks were seen in the night sky by the people .
2. The first rockets were made by the Chinese.
3. Rockets were used by the Arabs.
4. Boulogne was destroyed by the British army with rockets.
5. The buildings were burned by fires from the rockets.
6. Rockets were used by the Germans in World War 2.
7. Heavy rockets were developed by the Germans.
8. Many people were killed by the rockets.
9. Sputnik I was launched by the Russians in 1957.
10. Laika was sent into space.
11. The rockets were improved a lot by the British.
12. Sputnik was carried into orbit by strong rockets.
13. Radio sounds were sent back to Earth by Sputnik.
14. Sputnik II was launched a month later by the Russians.
15. Laika was called Mutnik by the people.
16. Rockets were developed by smart scientists.

EXERCISES 1 AND 2 – WORKBOOK PAGE 22

ACTIVITY 3:   **Divide into small groups. Role play the following scenarios:**

Write your conversation in a notebook, and be ready to role-play it for the class.

SCENARIO 1:
Some people in your group love animals. One person thinks it was cruel for the Montgolfier brothers to send a sheep, a duck and a rooster on the first flight of their balloon. Another person thinks it was wrong for the Soviets to send animals into space. Another person in the group thinks that the animal experiments were needed to test the safety of the equipment before humans were sent into space. Make a conversation about this.

SCENARIO 2:
Your group is talking about the Soviet space program and their use of dogs in their rockets. One person thinks that this should never be done. Another person points out that these were stray dogs that were living on the streets of Moscow. On the streets, the dogs would have a very bad time. It gets extremely cold in the winter, and they likely wouldn't get enough to eat. At the space center, they would be warm and well looked after. If they died in space, it wouldn't be as bad as dying of starvation or freezing to death. Make a conversation about this.

SCENARIO 3:
Your group is talking about the space race. Both United States and the Soviet Union spent billions of dollars on rockets and equipment for space. Some people think that this money should have been used to help the people on Earth, perhaps with cancer research, or feeding some of the hungry people in the world. Other people think that mankind should always be learning more about the world and the stars, and that we shouldn't think about the money. Make a conversation about this.

SCENARIO 4:
Your group is talking about countries exploring space. Some think that every country should be free to do as much as they want in space, and that we will all learn a lot about our world by this work. Others think that eventually, it could become dangerous. Sometime in the future some country might want to use space to make war on other countries. Make a conversation about this.

Postage stamp with Laika and
Sputnik II

EXERCISE 3 – WORKBOOK PAGE 23

VOCABULARY

leader	offer, to	brilliant	era
super power	joke, to	Cold War	hostile
revolution	Communism	democratic	
recruit. to	microchip		competition

ACTIVITY 1: **Listen to the audio and your teacher read the passage, then take turns reading orally.**

After the Second World War, the military leaders saw that the Germans had some very good rockets, and that they were working very hard to make better ones. People from the Soviet Union and the American governments went to Germany and found all of the leading German rocket scientists. They offered them very good jobs if

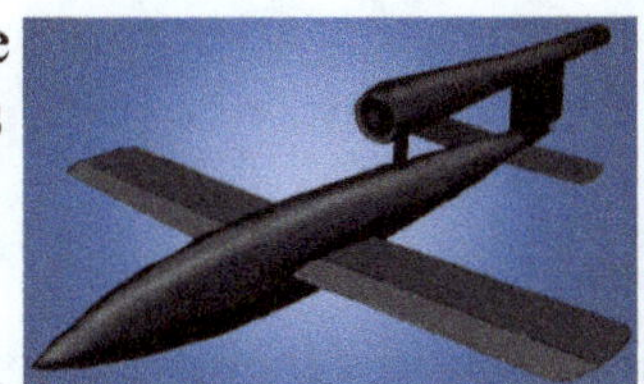

German V1 rocket

they would work for them. Many of these brilliant men and women went to the Soviet Union, and many went to America to live. Usually the era in history known as the "Space Race" is said to have started in 1957 when the Soviet Union launched Sputnik 1. Really, the Space Race began in 1945, when people from the two super powers went to Germany to recruit the German rocket scientists.

The American people were sure that America was the very best in rocket science, and that no one knew as much as they did about rockets. Because they had so many German rocket scientists working on their space program, people made a joke by saying: "Our German scientists are better than the Russian German scientists."

Then on the 4th of October 1957, the Soviet Union launched Sputnik I, and surprised the world.

During that time, the USSR and the United States were in the middle of the Cold War. It was called the Cold War, because there was no combat, but the countries were very hostile to each other. The USSR wanted the world to believe that the Communist revolution was very successful, and that they had the best of everything. The United States believed that their democratic system was the best.

The space race became a giant competition between the two governments, to show the world which country was the best.

ORAL QUESTIONS TEACHER'S GUIDE

EXERCISE 1 AND 2 – WORKBOOK PAGE 24
EXERCISE 3 – WORKBOOK PAGE 25

ACTIVITY 4:   **DEBATING**
SEATING   **Debating is the discussion of two points of view.**
                          A <u>moderator</u> organizes the discussions.

MODERATOR
STUDENTS   **Name of moderator**_________________

Divide into two groups.

Group 1 agrees with the statement.   **Group 2 doesn't agree with the statement.**
          We say they are "**Pro**"   We say they are "**Con**".

The statement to be discussed today is:
**The USSR and the USA should have worked together to explore space,
instead of having a space race.**

The moderator is between the groups but at one end.
The two groups are often referred to as **Pro** and **Con**.
Each group brainstorms and writes down
ideas that support what they think.

One person from each group
will present their group's ideas to the large group.

It is very important that the students
sit with the two groups facing each other.

Return to the large group

Moderator:
**The USSR and the USA should have worked together to explore space,
instead of having a space race.**

Moderator: Now we will hear from Group 1, speaking for the Pro side.
                          Now we will hear from Group 2, speaking for the Con side.

Now <u>everyone</u> in the room, except the Moderator, should say why they agree or disagree with the
statement. They are to think of as many things as they can. Unusual or funny ideas are very good.
Remember, you are learning English, not solving the problems of the world.

VOCABULARY

https://tinyurl.com/4dcmc69j

spectacular	failure	turtle	monkey
living	creature	travel	message
organize, to	victory	sub-orbital	achievement
person	praise, to	system	area
wait, to (waited)	gas	float, to	crisis
education	billion	defense	industry
1radiation	goal		

ACTIVITY 1: **Listen to the audio and your teacher read the passage, then take turns reading orally.**

Both the United States and the Soviet Union launched many rockets to learn about space. They found that there were many dangers. Some of the launches were spectacular failures. Both countries sent animals into space – dogs, turtles and monkeys. This was to see if living creatures could survive such a rocket flight. Manned flight was extremely dangerous.

On April 12th, 1961, Yuri Gagarin was the first human being to travel through space in an earth orbit. He made one orbit around the earth, lasting 108 minutes. His first message to Earth was:
"I see the earth! It's beautiful!"
When he landed, he praised the Government of the Soviet Union as being the "Organizer of all our victories."

On May 5th, 1961, just 23 days later, Alan Shepard made a sub-orbital flight for the United States. The flight was only 15 minutes in length, but they were able to test many of their systems.

The following year, on February 20th, 1962, John Glenn successfully orbited the earth three times. In 1962 this was a real achievement. They were able to place a living person into earth orbit, have him travel around the earth three times, and then land in an ocean safely in a place where Navy ships could find him.

Launching Friendship 7,
carrying John Glenn.
Photo courtesy of NASA.

At that time, the capsule which the astronauts were riding in landed in the ocean. There were many Navy ships in the area, waiting for the landing.

When the capsule hit the water, big balloons filled with gas, and kept the capsule floating while the Navy ships came to get the astronauts.

Astronauts being taken
from the capsule into a
small Navy boat
Photo courtesy of NASA

When the USSR launched Sputnik I, it frightened many people. In fact, in American history, it is known as the "Sputnik Crisis". Although the Russian rockets carried the satellite into orbit, it also meant that the Russians could send a bomb anywhere in America.

The Americans decided to improve their education system by spending over a billion dollars on education for the defense industry.

The Americans had some difficulties catching up to the Russians, but nearly four months after the Sputnik I launch, they launched their first satellite, Explorer I. They learned a lot about radiation that circles the earth with this satellite. Both the United States and the Soviet Union were working hard to learn as much as they could, because they both wanted to be able to put the first person on the moon. This was their goal.

ORAL QUESTIONS TEACHER'S GUIDE

ACTIVITY 2: You are talking with your friend about the space race.

Role-play this conversation.

You: We were reading about the Space Race on the internet. For a while in 1957 people were worried about what the military leaders in the Soviet Union would do.

Friend: What were they worried about? Sputnik I and II didn't

You: carry any bombs or anything like that.

Everyone was afraid that they would be able to use rockets to send nuclear bombs anywhere in the world. If they could send something into orbit, they could also bomb cities.

Friend: The Americans weren't very far behind, though, were they?

You: No, they weren't very far behind. They launched the first Explorer just about four months later. Both countries wanted to be able to put a person on the moon. This would show the world who was the best. Would you want to go to the moon?

Friend: Yes, I'd like to go to the moon.

EXERCISE 1 AND 2 – WORKBOOK PAGE 26
ACTIVITY 3 – WORKBOOK PAGE 27

VOCABULARY

footprint	carol	page	imply, to	strength
dusty	giant	benefit	withdraw, to	spacecraft
descend	lunar	face plate	hop, to	sample
gravity	reflection	popular	provide, to	scary
fuel	stranded	ridiculous	oxygen	breathe, to
North Pole	jungle			

https://tinyurl.com/37dmc9ne

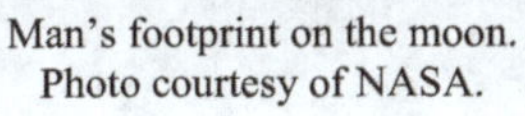

Man's footprint on the moon.
Photo courtesy of NASA.

ACTIVITY 1: Listen to the audio and your teacher read the passage, then take turns reading orally.

We often hear about "footprints". Sometimes people speak of "following in his father's footprints". Other people sometimes talk about "footprints in the sands of time."

In the famous Christmas Carol, the king, told the tired page to
walk in his footprints. This implies that the page boy would get strength from the footprints.

There is no footprint, however, as famous as the one above. This picture was taken by Edwin Aldrin on July 21st, 1969, showing one of man's very first steps in the dusty surface of the moon. Neil Armstrong, who was the first person to step on the moon said: "That's one small step for man, one giant leap for mankind."

The Apollo program, which carried the astronauts to the moonMoon was popular in the United States. It provided a great many jobs, and there were many benefits from the space research that helped science and industry in many different ways.

Meanwhile, the space program in the USSR had many difficulties. They withdrew from the race to the moon, but continued to do useful research in space travel.

Landing a spacecraft on the moon is a very difficult thing to do. Quite a few spacecraft were sent to fly past the moon before the Apollo 11 mission attempted this. Some of the flights had astronauts aboard, or "manned" flights, and some of them were "unmanned" flights. Some unmanned flights were designed to descend slowly to the surface of the moon, and then crash on the lunar surface. During their descent, these flights were taking pictures and sending them back to earth. There were also other instruments sending back all sorts of information about the moon.

As the astronauts collected rock samples to bring back to Earth, they moved about by hopping, because the moon gravity is only one sixth that of Earth. The picture below shows Aldrin stepping onto the lunar surface.

ACTIVITY 2:   Divide into small groups. Role play the following scenarios:

Scenario 1:
Your group is trying to imagine how it would feel to step onto the moon for the first time. Make a conversation about this.

Scenario 2:
Armstrong and Aldrin's families are watching the walk on the moon on television. What are they saying? Make a conversation about this.

Scenario 3:
You are the scientists and engineers back at the Space Center. You are very happy that the astronauts are able to walk on the moon. Make a conversation about this.

Photo courtesy of NASA.

ORAL QUESTIONS TEACHER'S GUIDE
EXERCISES 1 AND 2 – WORKBOOK PAGE 28
EXERCISE 3 AND 4 – WORKBOOK PAGES 29 AND 30

Lesson 14

VOCABULARY

tank	explode, to	impact	body	period	impressive
long-range	expensive	explore, to	solar system	gather, to	signal
atmosphere	magnetic field	giraffe	terrible	conditions	universe

ACTIVITY 1: Listen to the audio and your teacher read the passage, then take turns reading orally.

The moon landing by Neil Armstrong and his crew was just part of the very large Apollo program, which stretched from 1961 to 1972

Apollo 11 and 12 both landed men on the moon. Apollo 13 nearly ended in disaster. An oxygen tank exploded, but the crew, and all of the people back on Earth worked to save the mission. Because all the men returned safely to Earth, the mission was called a success.

Apollo Missions 14 to 17 all landed men on the moon, and brought back many samples and a great deal of information. Some of the rocks are as old as 4.6 billion years. Scientists believe that the moon was formed by the huge impact of a very large body hitting the earth.

At the time, President John Kennedy of the United States said: "No single space project in this period will be more impressive to mankind, or more important in the long-range exploration of space; and none will be so difficult or expensive to accomplish."

Pioneer 10 in space.   Photo courtesy of NASA

Starting in 1965, the Pioneer missions were designed to explore space. These missions were all unmanned.

The first Pioneer missions had many difficulties, but some progress in interplanetary exploration was made.

On March 2nd, 1972 Pioneer 10 was launched. Its goal was to learn about the planets in our solar system. It gathered a lot of information about Jupiter.

Pioneer 10 sent back enormous amounts of information about planetary atmospheres, magnetic fields, as well as many beautiful close up pictures of the planets. It passed Jupiter in December 1973, still sending information back to Earth.

On January 23rd, 2003, Earth received the last signal from Pioneer 10. At that time it was 12 billion kilometers from Earth. It is still traveling! It might reach the star Aldebran in 2 million years.

Pioneer 11 flew close to Saturn and Jupiter. It sent back the first pictures of Saturn's rings. It was last heard from in 1995, but it was still flying!

THE USE OF "TOO".
"Too" has two meanings:
It can mean **<u>also</u>**.
Example: Pioneer 11 flew past Saturn and Jupiter <u>too</u>.
It can suggest a **<u>negative result</u>**.
Example: Space exploration is <u>too</u> expensive for most countries.

ACTIVITY 2:   **Divide into groups of two or three.**
Join these sentences to make one sentence, using "too". Check your answers in the box.

1.   Pioneer 11 went close to Jupiter.
      Pioneer 11 went close to Saturn.

2.   I don't want to go to the moon.
      The moon is far away.

3.   Animals can't live on the moon.
      The moon is very hot in the day time.

4.   Lots of men go into space.
      There are women astronauts.

5.   Some planets we'll never visit.
      Some planets are very far away.

6.   Planes travel very fast.
      Rockets travel very fast.

7.   Edwin Aldrin walked on the moon.
      Neil Armstrong walked on the moon.

Earth seen from the moon.
Photo courtesy of NASA.

1. Pioneer 11 went close to Jupiter and Saturn too.

2. I don't want to go to the moon, it's too far away.

3. Animals can't live on the moon, it's too hot in the day time.

4. Lots of men go into space, but there are women astronauts, too.

5. Some planets we'll never visit, they are too far away.

6. Planes travel very fast, and rockets travel very fast, too.

7. Edwin Aldrin walked on the moon, Neil Armstrong walked on the moon too.

EXERCISE 1 AND 2 – WORKBOOK PAGE 31
EXERCISE 3 – WORKBOOK PAGE 32

ACTIVITY 4:   **DEBATING**
  SEATING   **Debating is the discussion of two points of view.**
A <u>moderator</u> organizes the discussions.

MODERATOR
STUDENTS   **Name of moderator________________**

Divide into two groups.

Group 1 agrees with the statement.   **Group 2 doesn't agree with the statement.**
We say they are "**Pro**"   We say they are "**Con**".

The statement to be discussed today is:
Satellites in space have been a great benefit to mankind.

The moderator is between the groups but at one end.
The two groups are often referred to as **Pro** and **Con**.
Each group brainstorms and writes down
ideas that support what they think.

One person from each group
will present their group's ideas to the large group.

It is very important that the students
sit with the two groups facing each other.

Return to the large group

Moderator: Satellites in space have been a great benefit to mankind.

Moderator: Now we will hear from Group 1, speaking for the Pro side.
Now we will hear from Group 2, speaking for the Con side.

Now <u>everyone</u> in the room, except the Moderator, should say why they agree or disagree with the statement. They are to think of as many things as they can. Unusual or funny ideas are very good. Remember, you are learning English, not solving the problems of the world.

Lesson 15

VOCABULARY

cluster	advantage	ultra violet	infra red	mirror	telescope
great deal	increase, to	surprise	recently	astronomer	point
light year	distant	gradually	born, to be	form, to	nebula

The Hubble Space Telescope
Picture courtesy of NASA.

https://tinyurl.com/ywamszvm

ACTIVITY 1: **Listen to the audio and your teacher read the passage, then take turns reading orally.**

On April 24th, 1990, NASA launched a rocket carrying the Hubble Space Telescope into orbit.

This was a very expensive mission, but there are a great many advantages to having a telescope in space. Because there is no atmosphere in space, the pictures are very clear, and ultra violet and infra red photography can be used very well.

It was soon found that the mirror in the telescope was made incorrectly. However, a great deal of useful work could still be done. Then in 1993, a space shuttle mission was sent to put in new equipment which corrected this problem.

Since that time, the Hubble Space Telescope has sent back thousands of amazing photographs from space. We are now able to see an enormous number of things that could never be seen from Earth. The Hubble Space Telescope has greatly increased our understanding of the universe.

Space dust seen in a nebula by the Hubble
Space Telescope.
Picture courtesy of NASA.

Even the people studying these things find that with the Space Telescope, they are having many surprises.

Just recently, two astronomers at the University of British Columbia in Canada discovered a cluster of several hundred stars. Although each of these clusters may contain hundreds of thousands of stars, each cluster was just a faint point of light in the picture sent back from the Hubble Telescope. This is because they are so far away. These clusters of stars are thought to be more than a billion light years away from Earth. (A light year is the distance that light can travel in one year.) These star clusters are thought to be the most distant things ever seen.

Because the light has taken a billion years to reach us, scientists are able to see these stars the way they looked a billion years ago. With the Hubble Space Telescope, astronomers and scientists can see how stars and solar systems were born. Gradually, over time, they are learning about how our universe was formed.

ORAL QUESTIONS TEACHER'S GUIDE

ACTIVITY 2:   **Listen to your teacher read this conversation, then role-play.**

Brian: Just think of the enormous distance! That light was traveling for a billion years to reach us. That's hard to imagine!

Pam: I can't even think of a distance like that. How much is a billion, anyway?

Ruth: A billion is a thousand millions, so a billion is a number so big, we can hardly think of it!

Ray: I just looked up the speed of light. It's 299, 792, 458 meters per second.

Brian: A billion light years! That's too much for me to think about. Let's go and have a coffee!

EXERCISES 2 AND 2 – WORKBOOK PAGE 33
ACTIVITY 3 – WORKBOOK PAGE 34

type	space station	international	load	material	site
transportation	part	solid rocket	booster	power	color
rust	external	carry, to	break, to	cargo bay	crew
separate, to					

ACTIVITY 1: Listen to the audio and your teacher read the passage, then take turns reading orally

The engineers and scientists at NASA needed another type of spacecraft. They planned to build an International space station in space. They needed a spacecraft that could carry loads of building materials into space, and come back for more. This is just like a truck going to a building site on Earth.

They designed and built the Space Transportation System. People now call it the Space Shuttle. All of the expensive parts can be used over and over again.

There are three parts to the space shuttle. There are two solid rocket boosters. These two rockets give the shuttle most of its power. There is a huge rust colored external tank, which carries a lot of fuel. The third part is the orbiter. This is the spacecraft that carries the crew, and the crew flies it back to land on Earth.

The shuttle has a huge cargo bay, measuring 4.6 by 18.3 meters, for carrying materials and equipment into space. There are usually 5 to 7 crew members on each flight.

Although this has been a very successful program, stretching from 1977 to the present, there were two flights that turned into disasters and the crews died.

Saturn's rings, with the cold moon Tethys in the background.

Picture taken by the Hubble Space Telescope.
Courtesy of NASA.

THE SPACE SHUTTLE

Two Solid Rocket Boosters

These two rockets supply most of the power for blast off.
They only fire for about two minutes. At that time, the shuttle
is about 45.7 kilometers above Earth. They break away from
the shuttle. Parachutes open, and they fall into the ocean.
They are picked up and used again

External Fuel Tank

About five minutes into flight, the huge external fuel tank
separates and falls towards earth. It becomes very hot in the
atmosphere and some of the remaining fuel in it causes it to
explode. The remaining pieces are very small and burn up in
the air.

Orbiter

This is the spacecraft that goes up into Earth orbit, and flies
back to earth. It has a huge cargo bay for carrying tools and
equipment into space. The rockets are controlled by five on
board computers for most of the flight.

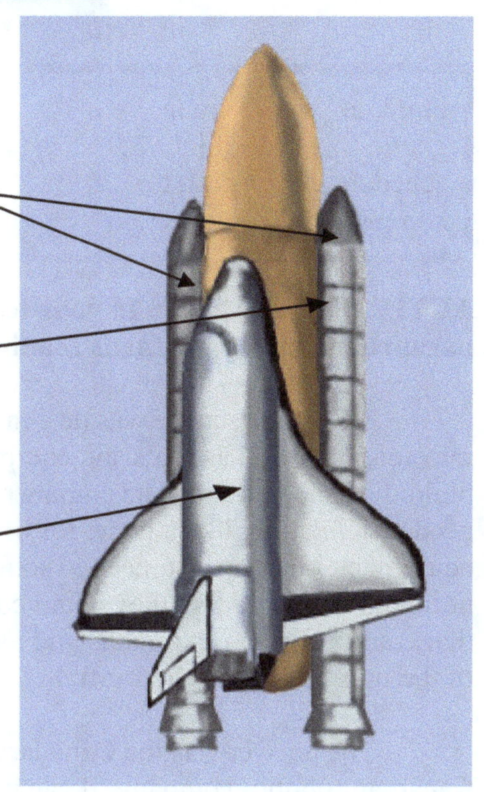

ORAL QUESTION TEACHER'S GUIDE

ACTIVITY 2:   **Divide into groups of two or three.**
Answer the questions in sentences. Check your answers in the box.

1.   During blast off which part of the shuttle does most
     of the lifting?
2.   What happens to the external fuel tank after it
     separates from the orbiter?
3.   Can the solid rocket boosters be used more than
     once?
4.   Where does the crew ride?
5.   What goes into the cargo bay?
6.   How long do the solid rocket boosters fire?
7.   Why do the solid rocket boosters have
     parachutes?
8.   When does the external fuel tank separate from
     the orbiter?
9.   Have all of the shuttle missions been successful?
10. How are the rockets controlled for most of the
     flight?

1.   The solid rocket boosters do most
     of the lifting.
2.   The external fuel tank explodes after
     separation.
3.   Yes, they can be used many times.
4.   The crew rides in the orbiter.
5.   Tools and equipment go in the cargo
     bay.
6.   The solid rocket boosters fire for
     about two minutes.
7.   They have parachutes to slow down
     their descent.
8.   The external fuel tank separated
     about five minutes into the flight.
9.   No, two of the missions ended in
     disaster.
10. The rockets are controlled by
     computers for most of the flight.

EXERCISE 1 – WORKBOOK PAGE 35
EXERCISES 2 and 3 – WORKBOOK PAGE 36

build, to	crane	carry, to	tool	robotics	brush, to
gentle	joint	shoulder	elbow	wrist	finger
schedule	test, to	fuel cell	shorten, to	excited	instead
complete, to	expect, to	enjoy, to	vacuum cleaner	clean, to	

ACTIVITY 1:   Listen to your teacher read the paragraphs, then take turns reading orally.

The space shuttle was designed to carry satellites into space, as well as tools and equipment needed to build the space station. The engineers decided they needed something like a crane for lifting the heavy equipment, but they also needed something more. They needed a huge arm that they could control from the orbiter that could carry the astronauts and tools to different parts of the outside of the spacecraft.

The answer was the Canadarm, developed by a Canadian robotics company. It can move heavy equipment, just like a very strong arm, and it can brush ice off the outside of the orbiter, just like gentle fingers.

The Canadarm works just like a strong arm and hand. It has six joints – two in the shoulder, one in the elbow, and three in the wrist.

The Canadarm first went into space in November of 1981. The crew had many jobs to do, and the last day they were scheduled to test the Canadarm. There was a problem with one of the fuel cells, so it was decided on Earth to shorten the mission and not test the Canadarm. The night before their return, the crew said "goodnight" to their controllers, and everyone thought they were going to sleep.

The crew were so excited about this new arm that instead of sleeping, they spent the night testing it. By morning, they had completed over 90% of the tests. They found that it could do much more than they expected, and they enjoyed using it.

https://tinyurl.com/2s3e93cz

Astronaut Jeffrey Hoffman with the equipment used to repair the Hubble Space Telescope. Photo courtesy of NASA.

ORAL QUESTIONS TEACHER'S GUIDE

ACTIVITY 2: Divide into small groups. Choose one of the scenarios below and make a conversation. Role-play your conversation for the class.

Scenario 1:
You are talking with your friends about robotics. You have read that many of the automobile companies use robots to do a lot of the work. They can work in unsafe places, and they don't get tired. One of your friends thinks that the jobs should all be done by people. Make a conversation about this.

Scenario 1:
You have just read that the Canadarm can reach into the cargo bay, and pick up heavy equipment just like a giant arm. It did this when it was used to repair the Hubble Space Telescope. It is controlled by an astronaut sitting inside the orbiter. You are telling your friends about it, and they are asking you questions. Make a conversation about this.

Scenario 3:
One of your group thinks that robots will soon be doing many of the jobs we don't like doing. Life will be easier then. Another of your friends doesn't think so. Someone invented a robot vacuum cleaner. It was made to go back and forth in a room from one side to the other, cleaning the whole room. There were very bad problems with it. It kept falling down the stairs! Make a conversation about this.

Scenario 4:
Your friends have seen pictures of astronauts riding on the Canadarm outside of the orbiter. Some of you think it would be wonderful, but others think it would be very scary. Make a conversation about this.

EXERCISE 1 – WORKBOOK PAGE 37
EXERCISE 2 – WORKBOOK PAGE 38

The Canadarm being tested on the night of its first flight.
Photos courtesy of NASA.

Astronaut Bruce McCandless going to work outside of the orbiter on the Canadarm.

mobile	rover	robot	damage, to	opportunity	spirit
amazing	study, to	crash, to	information	softly	possibly
dig, to	surface	controller	change, to	decide, to	storm
possibly	blow, to	cover, to	happen, to		

ACTIVITY 1: Listen to the audio and your teacher read the passage, then take turns reading .

A Mars Rover.
Photo courtesy of NASA.

After many manned missions to the moon, scientists decided to explore Mars. Because of the great distance, and the very difficult atmosphere on Mars, they decided that unmanned missions were the only way they could study Mars. There were a great many unmanned missions sent to Mars. Some orbited Mars, while others crashed onto the surface. These missions sent back a great deal of information.

Two mobile robots, called rovers, were sent to Mars in June and July, 2003. These rovers are the most successful missions ever accomplished.

They were called Spirit and Opportunity Landing the rovers on Mars was a big problem. It was necessary for the rovers to land without crashing, which would damage all of the equipment on them.

The scientists and engineers designed a landing capsule that would let the rovers land softly, then move out of the capsule safely, even if the capsule landed on a big rock.

Soon after landing, the rovers started moving across the very difficult surface of the planet. As they moved along, they took hundreds of pictures, and dug into the surface to find out what the planet's surface was like. All this information was sent back to Earth.

In January of 2004, the controllers on Earth found that there was a problem with the computer programs on Spirit. They spent ten days changing the programs, and Spirit was ready to start again. Then, to be sure, they made the same changes to the computer programs on Opportunity.

In March 2004, Scientists studying the information sent back by the rovers, decided that there was water on the surface of Mars, at one time. They also found that Mars could possibly have some forms of life on it today.

Sunset on Mars. Photo taken by a Mars Rover
courtesy of NASA.

Early in the mission there was a big dust storm. There was dust blowing all around the rovers for days. The scientists were sure that the dust would cover the solar panels and the rovers wouldn't be able to make enough electricity to do anything. When the storm was over, the rovers started work again as if nothing had happened.

Even though the rovers were expected to only go for about 90 days, they are still going! They are still sending back information about Mars, and may continue until 2010.

ORAL QUESTIONS TEACHER'S GUIDE

ACTIVITY 2:   **Listen to your teacher read the conversation, then role-play.**

You: Do you know anything about the Mars rovers
Opportunity and Spirit?

Friend: Yes, they're little robots that travel around on the surface
of Mars.

You: What are they doing there?

Friend: They're studying the surface of Mars and sending back a
lot of information and a lot of pictures.

You: Where do they get their power for this? Don't they run
out of fuel?

Friend: No, they have solar panels, so they can make electricity
from the sun.

You: When did they go to Mars?

Friend: They went there in the summer of 2003.

You: That's a long time! Did the scientists think they would continue working this long?

Friend: No, they thought they would only continue working for about ninety days.

You: That's amazing! They just keep getting power from the sun, and there's lots of that!

Friend: I guess they made them really strong so they would work on Mars.

EXERCISES 1 AND 2 – WORKBOOK PAGE 39

EXPRESSING THE FUTURE USING TIME CLAUSES

When a clause begins with a word that talks about a time in the <u>future</u> then the verb that follows the time clause uses the present <u>tense</u>.

A time clause will begin with words like the following:

when   before   after   as soon as   until   by the time

EXAMPLES:
The scientists <u>will want</u> all the information they can get about Mars <u>before</u> the rovers <u>stop</u>.
The shuttle <u>will take off</u> again <u>as soon as</u> they <u>can get</u> it ready.
The rovers <u>will go</u> <u>until</u> they <u>stop</u>.
The astronauts <u>will be</u> tired <u>by the time</u> they <u>get</u> home.

ACTIVITY 3: Divide into small groups. Answer the questions using time clauses. Check the box for the answers.

1. Will the astronauts come home when they finish their work in space?

2. When will the astronauts eat lunch?

3. When will the solid rocket boosters drop off the shuttle?

4. When will we hear of people going to the moon again?

5. Will we see pictures of the planets as soon as they are taken?

6. Will we hear about new stars as soon as they are discovered?

Astronaut moving equipment using the Canadarm.
Photo courtesy of NASA

1. Yes, they'll come home when they finish their work in space.
2. They'll eat lunch when they are hungry.
3. They will drop off when they are empty.
4. We will hear as soon as they go there.
5. Yes, we'll see pictures as soon as they are take
6. We'll hear about new stars as soon as they are

EXERCISES 3 - WORKBOOK PAGE 40

federation	agency	treaty	operate, to	laboratory	module
member	immediately	entire	continuously	solar panel	face, to
pipe	wire	zero	human body	sick	plant
push, to	float, to	pour, to	squeeze, to	toothpaste	tube

ACTIVITY 1:Listen to the audio and your teacher read the passage, then take turns reading.

On January 28, 1998 the United States, Canada, Japan, the Russian Federation, and 11 member states of the European Space Agency signed an international treaty to build and operate the International Space Station.

This is an orbiting laboratory where all of the member countries can do research. It was built in modules, or pieces, that were carried into space by either the space shuttle or the Russian Soyuz or Progress spacecraft.

Each module is designed to be used immediately after it is joined to the existing space structure. Astronauts have been living and working there continuously since November 2nd, 2000.

The International Space Station uses electricity that is made with its solar panels. As the space station moves, the solar panels turn, so that they are always facing the sun.

The International Space Station
Photo cortesy of NASA.

In space, there is no atmosphere, so there are no cloudy or rainy days to hide the sun.

As each piece or module of the space station is delivered, the astronauts have a lot of work to do to connect all of the pipes and wires that go from one part of the station to the new part.

Scientists are doing many experiments there to see how dangerous it is for people to be living in space. They are growing plants there, and they are studying the effects of radiation and zero gravity on the human body.

ACTIVITY 2: Divide into small groups. Choose one of the scenarios below and make a conversation. Role-play your conversation for the class.

Scenario 1:

You are talking about how it would feel to work in zero gravity. You might feel sick, or you might have trouble deciding which way was up. If you pushed a tool, you would have to hold on with your feet, or you would go flying backwards. All your tools would float around you. Make a conversation about this.

Scenario 2:

You and your friends are talking about how you would eat your meals if you were in the space station. If you put your food on a plate, it would float away. You couldn't pour a cup of coffee, because the coffee wouldn't pour. One of your group has read that the astronauts have their food in tubes, like toothpaste, and they just squeeze it into their mouths. Make a conversation about this.

Workers preparing medical research. Photo courtesy of NASA.

Astronaut David Wolf rides the Canadarm to work outside the space station, adding a new piece of equipment. Photo courtesy of NASA.

Scenario 3:

One of your group has read that the astronauts have little gardens in the space station. They are doing experiments to see how plants grow in zero gravity.

What do you think will happen? Maybe the astronauts will grow super plants that grow huge, because there is no gravity. What does your group think? Make a conversation about this.

Scenario 4:

The International Space Station is a wonderful way for the countries of the world to work together. About 25 % of the people of the world don't have clean water to drink. Make a conversation about this.

REVIEW LESSON

GERUNDS

**A gerund is the – ing form of the verb. It is used as a noun. It
is used in the same way as a noun – as a subject of an object.
Gerunds are used in sentences in three ways:**

1. The subject of a sentence:
<u>Flying</u> through the air would be fun.

2. The object of a verb:
I love <u>flying</u>.

3. The object of a preposition:
The birds were tired from <u>flying</u>.

ACTIVITY 1:   **Divide into small groups.**
Answer these questions using gerunds for the verb given. Then check your answers.

1.   Do you like swimming?
2.   Is reading one of your hobbies?
3.   Is eating too much bad for you?

1. Yes, I like swimming. No, I don't like swimming.
2. Yes, reading is one of my hobbies. No, it isn't one of my hobbies.
3. Yes, eating too much is bad for you.

CONDITIONAL SENTENCES

There are three words that are used for conditional sentences:

COULD – to be able   **WOULD -** expresses intention   **SHOULD** - duty

Conditional sentences use **could** to **express doubt**, so is often preceded by an "if" clause:
If I got home early I **could** help my mother.

Would is used to **ask politely** for something:
I **would** like coffee, please.

Should is used to **express a duty** to do something:
We **should** visit my aunt in the hospital.

CONDITIONAL SENTENCES: UNTRUE FACTS IN THE PRESENT TENSE
CLAUSE: A clause is a group of words that has a subject and a verb.

Clause 1	Clause 2
I would meet her at 7:00	if she weren't at work.

If the sentence **is untrue at the time**, use the **past tense** in the "if" clause.
"Were" is used for both singular and plural in conditional sentences.
If I were rich, I would buy a new car
If I were a dog, I would chase cats.

ACTIVITY 2:   Divide into small groups. Ask each other the questions, then check your answers.

1.   If you were rich would you be happy?
2.   If you had a car would you drive it?
3.   If you were a pilot would you fly a plane?

1.   Yes, if I were rich, I'd be happy No, if I were rich I wouldn't be happy.
2.   Yes, if I had a car I'd drive it.
3.   Yes, if I were a pilot, I'd fly a plane.

USING CONDITIONAL SENTENCES IN THE FUTURE TENSE

If the future tense **"will"** is used, put the **"if clause"** or the conditional clause, into the **present tense.**

EXAMPLES:
I will tell him <u>if</u> I **see** him.
He will understand <u>if</u> I **tell** him.
I'll buy a car when I **get** there.

ACTIVITY 3:   Divide into small groups. Ask each other the questions, then check your answers.

1. I will see you when I (to get)___________there.
2. I will cook some apples if I (to have) ___________them.
3. The children will run if they (to see) ___________me.

1. I will see you when I get there.
2. I will cook some apples if I have them.
3. The children will run if they see me.

SHOWING RELATIONSHIPS

<u>because</u> -   **is used to express expected results**

I eat dinner <u>because</u> I'm hungry.

<u>even though</u> or <u>although</u> are used to add an unexpected part (result) to a sentence.
I went to town, <u>even though</u> (although) I didn't want to buy anything.

<u>so</u> -   **is used to show that something is the result of something else**
I finished my work <u>so</u> I went home.

<u>but</u> -   **shows unexpected results**   **or**   **direct opposition**
He was sick <u>but</u> he went to work.   She was very poor <u>but</u> he was rich.

<u>but...anyway</u> -   **is used to show unexpected - opposite results.**
It was raining <u>but</u> they had a picnic <u>anyway</u>.

Lesson 20 Continued

ACTIVITY 4: Divide into small groups.

**Make sentences using <u>because</u>, <u>even though</u>, <u>although</u>, <u>so</u>, <u>but</u>, or <u>but…anyway</u>.
Then check for _possible_ answers in the box.**

1. they had many failures,   Orville and Wilbur kept trying
2. it was very dangerous,   the pilots kept flying
3. they kept working   Orville and Wilbur knew they could do it

1. Even though / although they had many failures, Orville and Wilbur kept trying.
2. It was very dangerous, but the pilots kept flying.
3. Orville and Wilbur knew they could do it so they kept working.

THE PASSIVE
The passive is used by using the verb "<u>to be</u>" plus the <u>past participle</u>

The passive is most often used when we don't know,
or when it is not important who does the action.

ACTIVE: (regular word order)   The Americans sent a satellite into orbit.
PASSIVE: A satellite <u>was sent</u> into orbit.

If it is important to know who does the action, "by" is used.

ACTIVE: (regular word order)   Good pilots flew the planes.
PASSIVE: The planes were flown by good pilots.

In the passive form, "to be" can be used in different tenses.
Lots of satellites were sent into orbit around the earth.
Lots of satellites are being sent into orbit around the earth.
Lots of satellites will be sent into orbit around the earth.

ACTIVITY 5:

**Divide into groups of two or three.
One person is to read the sentences. The other(s) are to give the passive form.
Check your answers in the box.**

1. People saw beautiful fireworks in the night sky.
2. The Chinese people made the first rockets.
3. The Arabs also used rockets

1. Beautiful fireworks were seen in the night sky by the people .
2. The first rockets were made by the Chinese.
3. Rockets were used by the Arabs.

THE USE OF "TOO".
"Too" has two meanings:
It can mean **also**.
Example: Pioneer 11 flew past Saturn and Jupiter <u>too</u>.
It can suggest a **negative result**.
Example: Space exploration is <u>too</u> expensive for most countries.

Divide into groups of two or three.

ACTIVITY 6:
Join these sentences to make one sentence, using "too". Check your answers in the box.

1. Pioneer 11 went close to Jupiter. Pioneer 11 went close to Saturn.
2. I don't want to go to the moon. The moon is far away.
3. Animals can't live on the moon. The moon is very hot in the day time.

1. Pioneer 11 went close to Jupiter and Saturn too.
2. I don't want to go to the moon, it's too far away.
3. Animals can't live on the moon, it's too hot in the day time.

EXPRESSING THE FUTURE USING TIME CLAUSES

When a clause begins with a word that talks about a time in the <u>future</u>
then the verb that follows uses the present <u>tense</u>.

A time clause will begin with words like the following:

when   **before**   **after**   **as soon as**   **until**   **by the time**

EXAMPLES:
The scientists <u>will want</u> to get all the information they can about Mars <u>before</u> the rovers <u>stop</u>.
The shuttle <u>will take off</u> again <u>as soon as</u> they <u>can get</u> it ready.
The rovers <u>will go</u> <u>until</u> they <u>stop</u>.
The astronauts <u>will be</u> tired <u>by the time</u> they <u>get</u> home.

ACTIVITY 7:   **Divide into small groups. Answer the questions using time clauses.**
Check the box for the answers.

1. Will the astronauts come home when they finish their work in space?

2. When will the astronauts eat lunch?

3. When will the solid rocket boosters drop off the shuttle?

1. Yes, they'll come home when they finish their work in space.
2. They'll eat lunch when they are hungry.
3. They will drop off when they are empty.

The History of Flight

Intermediate to Advanced ESL Lesson plans

Student Workbook

Lesson 1

EXERCISE 1:
Answer the questions in complete sentences:

1. Why could Mercury travel very fast?

   ____

2. How could the emperor in Persia see all parts of his kingdom?

   ____

3. Does ancient mythology have stories about creatures that could fly?

   ____

4. What was Pegasus?

   ____

ACTIVITY 3:   **Divide into small groups of two or three and complete this conversation.**
Role-play the finished conversation several times.

Narrator: You are talking with your friend about the history of flying.

You: Have you often wished that you were a bird, and could fly through the air?

Your Friend: Yes! I would ____

You: It must be interesting to people, because there are so many stories about flying.

Your Friend: Yes, in Persia____

You: There were lots of stories about flying carpets in Persia.

Your Friend: ____

You: In the old stories, people would sit on the magic carpet, then say some magic words, and the carpet would rise into the air and take them where they wanted to go. Wouldn't that be a lot of fun?

Your Friend: I guess so, but ____

You: Well, if you don't like the thought of a magic carpet, maybe you'd like to fly on the back of Pegasus.

Your Friend: ____

You: I think you would have to wait a few hundred years, and fly in an airplane. That would be safe.

EXERCISE 2: Crossword Puzzle:

ACROSS

1 its long and thin
6 goodness
7 a mythical beast
8 what birds fly with
9 the back of your foot

DOWN

1 something that means something else
2 a big bird
3 what kings and queens sit on
4 stories from the past
5 to be interested in

Lesson 2

EXERCISE 1: Answer the questions in sentences.

1.   What did the king ask Daedalus to build?

2.   What happened to Daedalus and Icarus after the maze was built?

3.   How did Daedalus and Icarus escape?

4.   What were the wings made of?

5.   Why did Icarus fall into the sea?

6.   Why didn't Daedalus like Perdix?

7.   Why didn't Perdix die when he was pushed off the tower?

8.   Why do people say that partridges don't like to fly too high?

EXERCISE 2:
Make sentences of the words below:

1.   Daedalus very called who was was man smart a There.

2.   fell melted sea wings, and The Icarus sun his into the.

3.   father and high He to his flew listen very didn't.

4.   his and hat little wings that he had was on It said heels

5.   a Greeks Pegasus called had flying horse The even.

6.   himself, feathers wax made wings for using two and big He.

7.   pushed Daedalus a high day, Perdix tower One off.

3

EXERCISE 3:
Fill in the blanks in the following paragraph using the adjectives given below:

Daedalus and Icarus lived in _________________ Greece. Daedalus worked for a

_________________ _________________ king. This king asked Daedalus to make

him a _________________ maze. He wanted it to be an _________________ place,

so that no one could ever find their way out. When it was finished, Daedalus was a

_________________man, because he was the _________________ person who knew

how to get out of the _________________ maze. The king didn't want Daedalus to tell

_________________ people, so he put him and his _________________ son Icarus

in prison. Daedalus was _________________ smart for the king. He made

_________________wings for himself and Icarus. One _________________ day

the _________________ Daedalus and Icarus flew over the _________________walls.

Icarus flew too close to the _________________ sun. He fell into the_________________
ocean.

USE THESE WORDS:

impossible	only	warm	ancient	huge	other
young	too	sunny	deep	other	beautiful
very	rich	happy	terrible	high	wise

EXERCISE 4: Write a short paragraph telling what you'd do if you had wings and could fly:

If I had wings and could fly____

____

____

____

____

Helpful Phrases:

fly like the wind	see all the sights	travel around the world
fly as high as I wanted	go to exotic places	wouldn't care about anything

EXERCISE 4:

MATCH THE MEANING
Write the correct meaning beside the words, using the definitions seen below:

myth ____

partridge ____

garden ____

tower ____

feather ____

escape ____

throne ____

righteousness ____

dragon ____

nephew ____

maze ____

prison ____

USE THESE WORDS:

your sister's son	a king or queen sits on it	stories from long ago
a place of flowers and bushes	a very high building	to get away
birds have them on their wings	goodness	a mythical creature
a bird	where they put bad people	a big puzzle

EXERCISE 1: Answer the questions in sentences.

1. What did the Montgolfier brothers build?

    ____

2. What did they put in their first balloon?

    ____

3. Did the duck, the sheep, and the rooster fly through the air?

    ____

4. What important people watched the two brothers on their first flight?

    ____

5. Where did they get the hot air to make the balloon rise?

    ____

6. What did the brothers think caused the balloon to rise?

    ____

7. Do you think their balloon flights were dangerous?

    ____

8. The Montgolfier brothers went up in their balloon in 1783. Do people still go up in balloons?

    ____

EXERCISE 2:   **Put the word in brackets ( ) into the correct tense.**

1. If I (to have) ____________________a chicken, I would eat it.

2. I would ride my bicycle if I (to have) ____________________it with me.

3. Maria would phone you tonight if she (to be) ____________________at home.

4. You could see a movie if you (to have) ____________________time.

5. If I (to be) ____________________you, I wouldn't do that.

6. If you (to be) ____________________rich would you be happy?

7. If I (to be) ____________________king, you could be my queen.

8. If we (to have) ____________________wings, we could fly.

9. If you (to see) ____________________her, you would like her.

10. He would be angry if he (to be) ____________________here.

11. If I (to have) ____________________the money, I would buy some coffee.

Student Workbook

ACTIVITY 3:   **BINGO**

Before playing the game the students are to write the numbers of the words in LIST 1
beside the words with the same meaning in LIST 2.

LIST 1   **MATCH THE MEANING**

1	**prison**	7	partridge	13	fascinate	19	beautiful
2	tower	8	dragon	14	snake	20	messenger
3	righteousness	9	nephew	15	heel	21	mind
4	myth	10	garden	16	ancient	22	to heal
5	maze	11	throne	17	symbol	23	shine
6	feather	12	escape	18	kingdom	24	to fly

LIST 2   **WORDS TO CALL:**

to move through the air	**1 where they put bad people**
it stands for something else	to interest
the back of your foot	stories from long ago
a long thin creature	birds have them on their wings
very pretty	a very high building
he carries messages	a place of flowers and bushes
your brother's son	you think with it
very old	a bird
a king or queen sits on it	to make better
what the sun does	to get away
where the king rules	goodness
a big puzzle	a mythical creature

<table>
<tr><td></td><td></td><td></td><td></td><td></td></tr>
<tr><td></td><td></td><td></td><td></td><td></td></tr>
<tr><td></td><td></td><td>**BINGO**
FREE</td><td></td><td></td></tr>
<tr><td></td><td></td><td></td><td></td><td></td></tr>
<tr><td></td><td></td><td></td><td></td><td></td></tr>
</table>

Lesson 4

ACTIVITY 2: Divide into groups of two or three. Make a conversation about early flight.

You: I just read about the first people who really did fly through the air. It wasn't
       Daedalus and Icarus.

Your friend: ____ ?

You: It was the Montgolfier brothers in France. They did it for King Louis XVI and his
       wife Josephine.

Your friend: ____ ?

You: No, they didn't make wings, they made a balloon. They lit a fire under the balloon
       and it rose into the air. They thought it was the smoke that caused the balloon to rise,
       so they made a very smoky fire.

Your friend: ____ ?

You: No, it wasn't their first balloon, a couple of months before they put a sheep, a duck
       and a rooster in a balloon and made it fly.

Your friend: ____ ?

You: No, the king didn't enjoy it. The book says that the wind blew the smoke in the
       king's face, and he was not at all happy about it.

EXERCISE 1: Answer in sentences.

1. When were the Chinese people making kites?

  ____

2. Was Leonardo da Vinci interested in flying?

  ____

3. Did George Caley fly in his gliders?

  ____

4. Did Caley fly a model with a small engine?

  ____

5. Did Otto Lilienthal make many flights?

  ____

6. Did Lilienthal have a motor in his planes?

  ____

7. Were Lilienthal's flights dangerous?

  ____

8. Why did Lilienthal stop flying?

  ____

EXERCISE 2: Crossword Puzzle:

ACROSS

3 he flies a plane
4 a plane with no motor
10 it makes things go
11 not true
13 to fix
14 a very light gas
15 about God

DOWN

1 it goes up in the air
2 the Chinese made them long ago
5 to write down
6 very surprising
7 you turn it
8 a small copy of something
9 wreck
12 towards the sky

Lesson 5

EXERCISE 1:   **Make correct sentences of the following words:**

1.   the, time, will, to, have, go, if, I, I, library

2.   phone, am, you, late, will, If, I, I

3.   London, money, I, had, I, fly, enough, if, would, to

4.   I, I, if, him, would, him, tell, saw

5.   see, ask, will, her, I, if, I, her

6.   were, He, if, wouldn't, alone, there, he, go

7.   early, car, I, I, the, If, home, wash, get, could

8.   high, If, I, wouldn't, were, so, Icarus, I, fly

9.   if, at, I, weren't, would, work, visit, she, her

10.   question, it, the, isn't, This, last, is?

EXERCISE 2:   **Answer the questions in sentences.**

1.   Were Zeppelins the first flying machines to carry passengers?

2.   Who had the first patent on Zeppelins?

3.   Did Zeppelins ever carry passengers across the Atlantic Ocean?

4.   Were Zeppelins used during the First World War?

5.   Who started the first airline company in the world?

10

EXERCISE 3:

MATCH THE MEANING
Write the correct meaning beside the words, using the definitions seen below:

wealthy   _______________________________________

transatlantic   _______________________________________

scenario   _______________________________________

reconnaissance   _______________________________________

enemy   _______________________________________

airline   _______________________________________

destination   _______________________________________

enormous   _______________________________________

accident   _______________________________________

to attempt   _______________________________________

glider   _______________________________________

hydrogen   _______________________________________

USE THESE WORDS:

very large
crosses the Atlantic ocean
where you are going person
or people against you

a company that has
airplanes something bad
that happens possible
situation
a plane with no motor

to try
exploration for information a
very light gas
have a lot of money

ACTIVITY 3: **Make a conversation between you and your friend about Wilbur and Orville Wright's work with airplanes.**

You: I read somewhere that the Wright Brothers were thinking of making a car before they got interested in flying.

Your Friend: ____

You: Because they thought that people wouldn't want to buy a car.

Your Friend: ____

You: Yes, they really were wrong about that. If they had worked on a car, do you think that other people would have made an airplane?

Your Friend: ____

You: Yes, I guess so. Do you know that very few people knew about their first flight?

Your Friend: ____

You: No, there were no reporters from the newspapers. There was one man that saw it all, though. His name was Amos Root. He had a journal for bee keepers called "Gleanings in Bee Culture". He wrote: "…these two brothers have probably not even a faint glimpse of what their discovery is going to bring to the children of men." He was right! No one knew what uses the airplane would have in the future.

Your Friend: ____

You: It used to take a long time to cross the ocean in a ship.

Your Friend: ____

You: Yes, it has changed international business a lot.

Your Friend: ____

____

____

You: The New York Times newspaper said that maybe in one million to ten million years people might be able to make a plane that would fly. Eight days later they did fly their plane! They fooled them, didn't they?

Caley's model plane

EXERCISE 1:   **Answer the questions in sentences:**

1.   How do you think Orville and Wilbur felt when their plane took off?

____

2.   Their first flight at Kitty Hawk broke the wing of their plane. Why do you think they kept trying?

____

3.   Do you think their work with early airplanes was dangerous?

____

4.   They read all of Otto Lilienthal's books on gliders. Do you think that this helped them?

____

5.   They must have been very smart, don't you think?

____

6.   Has air transportation changed what kind of food we eat?

____

7.   Do a lot of people use airplanes for traveling on business?

____

8.   Why did they have to build their own engine for their first plane?

____

9.   The New York Times newspaper said that they didn't think people would be able to make a plane that would fly. Why do you think they said that?

____

10.   Would you like to fly in one of the early planes?

____

EXERCISE 2:   **Fill in the blanks with the words given below.**

The brothers worked very hard and had some ________________ times. It was December 17th 1903,

an historic day. They put the track on some ________________ ground and used the wind to

________________ the plane along it. Orville was the ________________ while Wilbur ran beside it to

steady the ________________. The plane lifted off the ________________ for 12 seconds and flew for

120 feet. It was one of the great ________________ of the century.

USE THESE WORDS:

wing	**pilot**	**move**	**events**
difficult	**flat**	**ground**	

EXERCISE 3: Crossword Puzzle.

ACROSS

6 a person who writes for a newspaper or magazine

7 rich
11 car
13 the Wright's engine had four
14 a magazine
15 to make something go faster
16 very big

DOWN

1 power
2 slight
3 standing straight up
4 a quick look
5 to put back together
8 it spins
9 to find out about something
10 to go round and round
11 a person who flies planes
12 worry

Lesson 7

EXERCISE 1: Fill in the missing words from the list below.

The first _____________________ planes were used for ___________________ . When the

pilots saw other pilots, they ___________________ to them. Soon, the pilots starting throwing

things at the other pilots. Then they __________________ that the planes could be a very good

way to kill the ___________________ . They put heavy ___________________ in the

planes, so they could shoot down the enemy planes. Often a plane would chase another plane for a

long time, trying to get close enough to __________________ the other one down. It was like a

very __________________ game they were playing, and if you lost, you

__________________ . Some pilots shot down many planes before they were

___________________ killed.

USE THESE WORDS

finally	machine guns	shoot	decided
reconnaissance	waved	military	dangerous
enemy	died		

EXERCISE 2: Answer the questions in sentences.

1. What were the first military planes used for?

    ____

2. Did the soldiers on the ground sometimes shoot at the enemy planes?

    ____

3. Were the first pilots friendly to the enemy pilots?

    ____

4. Were many of the pilots killed in the war?

    ____

5. Did the military use zeppelins during the first war?

    ____

6. Do you think the Wright brothers thought that airplanes would be used in warfare when they
    started to build their first airplane?

    ____

EXERCISE 3:

MATCH THE MEANING
Write the correct meaning beside the words, using the definitions seen below:

unfortunately ____

military ____

prediction ____

risky ____

invention ____

aircraft ____

grenade ____

weapon ____

eventually ____

hero ____

bravery ____

observation ____

USE THESE WORDS:

the making of something new	finally	unluckily
looking at something carefully	a flying vehicle	a very brave person a
to do with the armed forces	to tell about the future not	bomb that is thrown
something you fight with	being afraid	dangerous

EXERCISE 4:   **Join the two sentences into one sentence,
using <u>because</u>, <u>even though</u>, <u>although</u>, <u>so</u>, <u>but</u>, or <u>but…anyway</u>.**

1. The New York Times didn't think it was possible for people to fly.
    Wilbur and Orville Wright made an airplane.

    ____

2. There were many disappointments.
    The brothers kept working.

    ____

3. The Wright brothers thought about building an automobile.
    They decided that no one would want to buy one.

    ____

4. They needed to study different wing shapes.
    They built a wind tunnel.

    ____

5. Their model planes kept crashing in the wind tunnel.
    They kept making new ones.

    ____

6. No one thought that people could ever fly.
    Orville and Wilbur fooled them.

    ____

7. Orville and Wilbur were very peaceful people.
    The military turned their invention into a weapon of war.

    ____

8. Flying an airplane in the war was very dangerous.
    Lots of young men wanted to do it.

    ____

9. The Wright brothers couldn't find a gas engine light enough to drive an airplane.
    They had to build their own engine.

    ____

10. Some planes were shot down by soldiers on the ground.
    The greatest risk was being shot down by other pilots.

    ____

Lesson 8

EXERCISE 1: You and your friend are talking about the early pilots in the First World War. Make a conversation.

Your Friend: I read that what Captain Dickenson said was true, when he made a prediction about warfare in the air.

YOU: ____

Your Friend: Yes, he said that at first the first planes would be used for reconnaissance. From the air, you could see where the enemy was, and what they were doing, but later, there would be fighting in the air.

YOU: ____

Your Friend: That's very interesting. The planes were open, and it was very easy for the pilots to see each other. So, as the planes passed each other, the pilots would wave.

YOU: ____

Your Friend: It is strange, isn't it? Later, they started to carry rocks and even grenades in their planes, so they could throw them at the other pilots. Finally, like Captain Dickenson predicted, they carried guns with them.

YOU: ____

Your Friend: Yes. Some of the pilots became very good at it. They also had the soldiers on the ground shooting at them. A number of the first pilots became great heroes because of their bravery. It was very dangerous, and quite a few men were killed.

EXERCISE 2:   **Answer the questions in sentences:**

1.   What was the Red Baron's elite flying group called?

____

2.   Flying over enemy lines was very risky, wasn't it?

____

3.   Do you think the Red Baron was a very good pilot, or was he just lucky?

____

4.   Do you think the Red Baron was happy about his success, or do you think he worried about all the men he killed?

____

EXERCISE 3: Crossword Puzzle.

ACROSS

3 to go after and try to catch
5 to work hard because you really want something
6 to take something given
9 a person, a thing, or a group 10 to get something by working for it 11 the very best
12 finally
13 things you need to work with

DOWN

1 the main office
2 pilot
3 fighting
4 where combat takes place 7 a plane with three wings
8 someone who is very good at something

Lesson 9

EXERCISE 1: Make good sentences with the words below.

1. to Chinese People rockets the were the first use that think.

    ____

2. 1000 AD before were using They likely rockets.

    ____

3. rockets the Boulogne with destroyed French The town of British.

    ____

4. Sputnik I to used The powerful launch Russians a rocket.

    ____

5. start Age launch of of Sputnik I Space was the the The.

    ____

6. do things that showed the Soviets they could The world great.

    ____

7. no afraid Even people carried weapons, it though made Sputnik.

    ____

8. to up The to work hard Americans had catch.

    ____

9. Earth it sent radio orbited waves as Sputnik back.

    ____

EXERCISE 2: Fill in the blanks, using the words below.

We think that rockets were _________________________ in China more than three thousand years

_________________________. They were used a lot by _________________________ forces to start fires.

They _________________________ scared people, too. During World War 2, Hitler had scientists work

on _________________________ for a long time. They made several kinds of rockets that they sent to

England with _________________________ in them. These rockets killed a lot of people.

Then, in 1957, the USSR _________________________ the world. It launched Sputnik. This was a

very small _________________________, but it circled the earth every 98 minutes and sent radio

messages back to Earth.

USE THESE WORDS:

military   always   bombs   rockets   developed   surprised   satellite   ago

20

ACTIVITY 3:   **BINGO**
Before playing the game the students are to write the numbers of the words in LIST 1
beside the words with the same meaning in LIST 2.

LIST 1   **MATCH THE MEANING**

1	**chase**	7	headquarters	13	glare	19	anthem
2	accept	8	combat	14	satellite	20	radio wave
3	unit	9	aviator	15	launch	21	to develop
4	finally	10	battlefield	16	canon ball	22	accomplish
5	earn	11	triplane	17	nuclear bomb	23	weapon
6	elite	12	ace	18	to orbit	24	risky

LIST 2   **WORDS TO CALL:**

it comes from a radio   **1   to go after and try to catch**

it orbits the earth   fighting
eventually   something very bright
flyer   a plane with three wings
to get something by working for it   the very best
to take something given   the main office
a very dangerous bomb   a kind of song
to send off   a person, thing, or group
where combat takes place   to finish
to circle   to change and grow or improve
it comes from a canon something   dangerous
to fight with   someone very good at something

<table>
<tr><td></td><td></td><td></td><td></td><td></td></tr>
<tr><td></td><td></td><td></td><td></td><td></td></tr>
<tr><td></td><td></td><td>BINGO
FREE</td><td></td><td></td></tr>
<tr><td></td><td></td><td></td><td></td><td></td></tr>
<tr><td></td><td></td><td></td><td></td><td></td></tr>
</table>

21

Lesson 10

EXERCISE 1:
Make a conversation with your friend. Write what "You" would say

Friend: We have come a long way since the first flight
by the Wright brothers, haven't we?

You: ______________________________________

____

Friend: People fly all around the world, in fast planes,
and aren't the rockets of today different?

You: ______________________________________

Friend: Poor Laika! It must have been a terrible trip in Sputnik II!

You: ______________________________________

Friend: Do you think Laika would have been able to live through the winter on the streets of
Moscow?

You: ______________________________________

Friend: When Sputnik II ran out of air, Laika probably just went to sleep and then died in her
sleep. That wasn't too bad.

You: ______________________________________

EXERCISE 2:   **Answer the questions in sentences.**

1. Was the United States the first country to put a satellite into orbit?

____

2. Did Laika go in the first satellite?

____

3. Why did they send a dog into space?

____

4. Why did Khrushchev want the second satellite launched so soon after the first?

____

5. Did the Soviets have other dogs in their space program?

____

6. What happened to the dog called Bold?

____

EXERCISE 3: Crossword Puzzle.

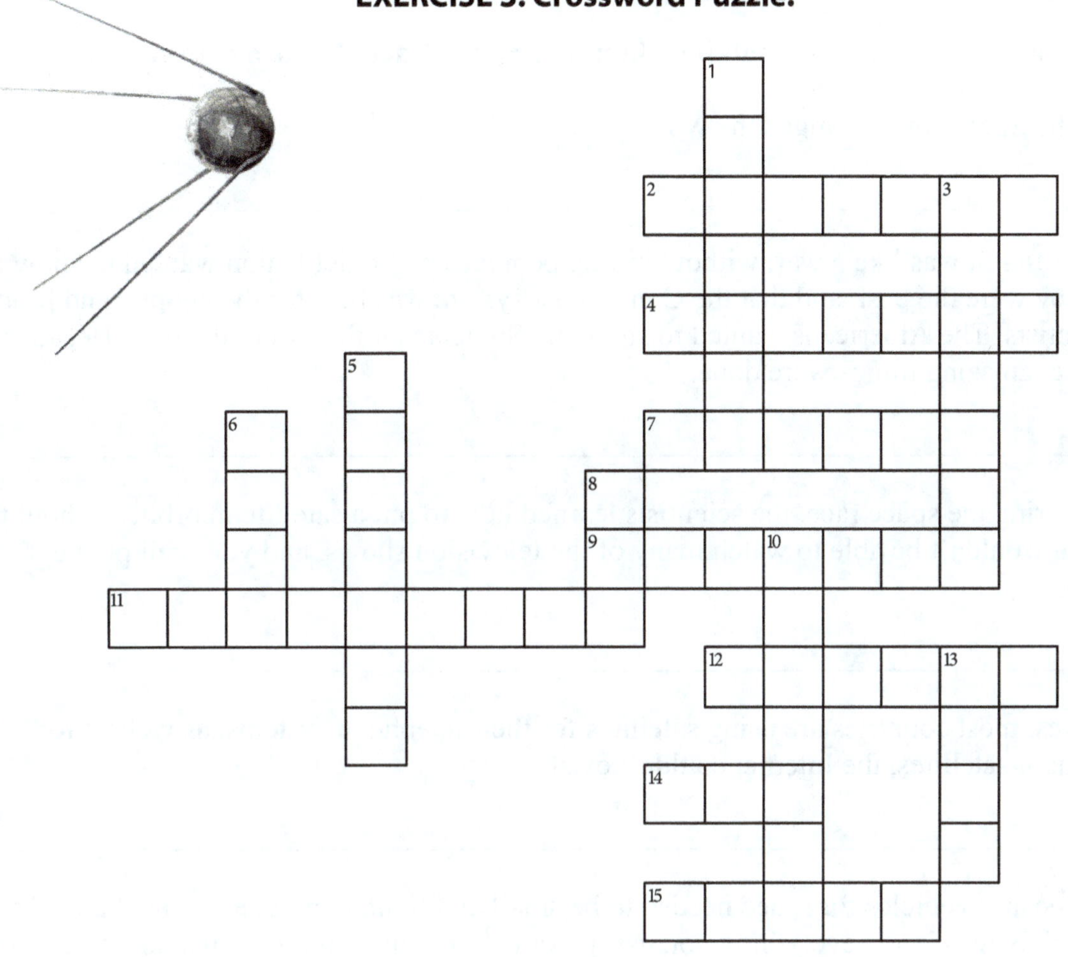

ACROSS

2 a plan for doing things
4 what has happened
7 to go back
9 what the astronauts travel in
11 it goes around the earth
12 to take something that is given
14 to stop living
15 dangerous

DOWN

1 to stay alive
3 to get things ready
5 eventually
6 another name for dog
8 someone very good at something
10 you get what you worked for
13 a way to get what you want

23

Lesson 11

EXERCISE 1:
> **You and your friend are talking about the Space Race. Make a conversation.**

You: The Space Race changed the world forever, didn't it?

Friend: ____

You: At first it was like a war, without killing people. The Soviet Union wanted to show the world that they were the best, and that the Communist system was best for the people, and produced the best scientists. The Americans wanted to show the Soviets that they were the best. Because of the space race, amazing things were done.

Friend: ____

You: During the space race, the scientists learned how to put a satellite in orbit. Without the satellites, you wouldn't be able to watch many of the television shows, and your cell phone wouldn't work.

Friend: ____

You: Yes, most countries are using satellites for their telephone systems, as well as for cell phones. Without satellites, the Internet couldn't exist.

Friend: ____

You: Because vehicles for space needed to be small and light, computers were changed to meet this need. Now, almost everything you use at home has a tiny microchip inside it to control how it works. This came from Space Race research.

EXERCISE 2:
During the Space Race the scientists learned to make everything small and light, so that they could carry their equipment in the spacecraft. We now have tiny chips in many of our household appliances. Can you name ten things that you find in most households that contain chips? (HINT: Often the chips are in the clocks.) Write the answers below:

1. ____________________________   2. ____________________________

3. ____________________________   4. ____________________________

5. ____________________________   6. ____________________________

7. ____________________________   8. ____________________________

9. ____________________________   10. ____________________________

EXERCISE 3:

MATCH THE MEANING
Write the correct meaning beside the words, using the definitions seen below:

leaders ____

revolution ____

prediction ____

offer ____

to joke ____

brilliant ____

era ____

hostile ____

competition ____

to return ____

bravery ____

blast off ____

USE THESE WORDS:

a fight to change government	a time in history	to say something funny
very smart	people follow them	to go back
one side tries to beat the	to tell about the future not	when a rocket takes off
other very unfriendly	being afraid	to give someone a chance

Lesson 12

EXERCISE 1: Answer the following questions in sentences.

1.   Both countries spent huge amounts of money on the Space Race. Do you think it was a good idea to spend the money that way? (Give the reasons for your answer.)

     ____

2.   What were the governments really interested in with their space programs?

     ____

3.   Both the USA and the Soviet Union were sending spacecraft into orbit. Why do you think they didn't work together?

     ____

4.   Both countries wanted to show the world that they were the best. Do you think putting an astronaut on the moon was a suitable way to prove that they were the best?

     ____

5.   Do you think that someday people will live on other planets?

     ____

EXERCISE 2: Use the words below to make good sentences.

1.   up, Soviet, was, but, the, Union, Americans, ahead, The, caught.

     ____

2.   times, earth, around, Shepard, flew, the, three, Alan.

     ____

3.   the, Yuri, in, a, great, Union, hero, Soviet, became, Gagarin.

     ____

4.   many, for, Space, brought, Research, Race, benefits, the.

     ____

5.   war, for, use, The, space, wanted, leaders, weapons, to, military, of.

     ____

6.   accidents, there, dangerous, many, flights, were, because, were, Space.

     ____

7.   a, Could, such, rocket, living, survive, flight, creatures?

     ____

ACTIVITY 3:   **BINGO**

Before playing the game the students are to write the numbers of the words in LIST 1
beside the words with the same meaning in LIST 2.

LIST 1   **MATCH THE MEANING**

1	**leaders**	7	era	13	program	19	satellite
2	revolution	8	hostile	14	history	20	to accept
3	prediction	9	competition	15	success	21	capsule
4	offer	10	to return	16	survive	22	dangerous
5	to joke	11	bravery	17	to die	23	prepare
6	brilliant	12	blast off	18	finally	24	ace

LIST 2   **WORDS TO CALL:**

someone very good at something   to get things ready
a plan for doing things   to go back
to say something funny   to stop living
not being afraid   when a rocket takes off
to stay alive   to give someone a chance
1. people follow them   you get what you worked for
to take something that is given   eventually
one side tries to beat the other   time
very unfriendly   a fight to change government
to tell about the future   risky
what has happened   smart
what the astronauts travel in   it goes around the earth

		BINGO **FREE**		

27

USING "GET" PLUS AN ADJECTIVE

"Get" is used with an adjective in a number of tenses.

EXAMPLES: Neil Armstrong got excited when they stepped on to the moon.
I get tired in the evenings.
If you don't eat you will get hungry.

EXERCISE 1:   Complete the sentences with the correct tense of "get".

1.   The astronauts ___________________ busy learning how to walk in a space suit.

2.   The astronauts thought that they ___________________ hungry if they didn't eat.

3.   The spacecraft ___________________ ready to blast off.

4.   They ___________________ safely back to earth after their long flight.

5.   Some companies ___________________ rich building space craft.

6.   Armstrong had a bag of rocks that ___________________ heavy.

7.   The astronauts ___________________ sleepy traveling back to Earth.

8.   It was ___________________ cloudy before they left.

9.   Their families were ___________________ worried when they were returning.

10.   The engineers were ___________________ happier by the minute.

EXERCISE 2: Answer the questions in sentences:

1.   Why was the Apollo Program popular in the United States?

____

2.   Did the USSR continue with the race to the moon?

____

3.   Why did Armstrong say it was a "giant leap for mankind"?

____

4.   Did some unmanned flights crash on the lunar surface?

____

5.   What did the astronauts collect on the moon?

____

EXERCISE 3:
You and your friend are talking about the Apollo mission to the moon. Make a conversation and then role-play.

Friend: That must have been pretty scary. I'd be too frightened to go to the moon.

You: _______________________________________

____

Friend: Maybe we would run out of fuel, or maybe the spacecraft would break down and leave me stranded on the moon.

You: _______________________________________

Friend: No, it's not ridiculous! How do they know how much fuel it would take to go to the moon?

You: _______________________________________

Friend: Well, there are all kinds of other risks. I wouldn't like it at all!

You: _______________________________________

Friend: I know that NASA sent lots of unmanned missions to study the moon, but it could be very different for people walking around on the moon.

You: _______________________________________

Friend: There's no air up there on the moon. Wouldn't it be awful if we went to the moon and there wasn't enough oxygen for us to breathe?

You: _______________________________________

Friend: What if the rockets didn't work properly? You really can't be sure. Then when you wanted to come home, the capsule might land at the North Pole, or in the jungle of Africa, or somewhere awful.

You: _______________________________________

Friend: Yes, I guess you're right! I just like to stay at home.

You: _______________________________________

Apollo 11 leaving for the moon.
Photo courtesy of NASA.

EXERCISE 4: Crossword Puzzle.

ACROSS

 3 frightening
 5 full of dust
 7 what you see in a mirror
10 to go down
12 to do with the moon
13 what you breathe
14 help
16 it pulls you down
17 astronauts fly them
18 well liked
19 to go somewhere

DOWN

 1 stupid
 2 a kind of fuel
 3 a small bit
 4 it makes an engine go
 6 left behind
 8 mark made by your foot
 9 very large
11 amazing to watch
15 you don't succeed

EXERCISE 1:   **Make a conversation. You are with your friend.**
You are talking about other forms of life in the universe.

You: There are lots of science fiction books that have terrible aliens living on other planets. Do you think we'll find other creatures in space?

Friend: ____

You: There might be some very strange forms of life in the universe, we don't know. People could hardly believe their eyes when they saw a giraffe for the first time.

Friend: ____

You: Yes, but we have some forms of life that live at the bottom of the ocean. They live very well under terrible conditions. They have lived there for hundreds of years.

Friend: ____

You: I wouldn't be sure of that! In some science fiction books there are aliens from other planets living right here, but we don't know about them.

Friend: ____

EXERCISE 2:   **Answer the questions in sentences:**

1.   Do you think that there are other forms of life in the universe?

    ____

2.   Did the Apollo missions discover any life on the moon?

    ____

3.   Why didn't the Apollo 13 mission land on the moon?

    ____

4.   Did Explorer 10 land on the moon?

    ____

5.   Did the scientists find out anything about how the moon was formed from the lunar landings?

    ____

6.   Is Pioneer 10 still flying away from the earth?

    ____

31

EXERCISE 3:

MATCH THE MEANING
Write the correct meaning beside the words, using the definitions seen below:

tank ____

long-range ____

atmosphere ____

to explode ____

expensive ____

impact ____

giraffe ____

to explore ____

solar system ____

terrible ____

period ____

universe ____

USE THESE WORDS:

the sun and bodies orbiting it an animal with long legs to fly apart with a noise very bad

it costs a lot to travel for discovery stretching into the future you carry liquids or gases in it

a length of time the gases around a planet when one thing hits another everything in space

Lesson 15

EXERCISE 1:   **Fill in the blanks, using the words below:**

_________________ the beginning of _________________, mankind has looked up and

watched the _________________ .

Many years _________________ the Greeks held their first Olympic games when Venus

was in a certain place in the _________________ . That was every four _________________ .

When we got _________________ rockets, scientists could _________________ the

moon, space, and some of the _________________ . Now we know what the _________________

is like on the planets. The _________________ that the _________________ brought back

from the _________________ told the a lot about the early days of the _________________ .

From all of the space _________________ we now know a lot more about our world.

USE THESE WORDS

scientists	astronauts	planets	powerful	ago
years	atmosphere	time	sky	stars
rocks	exploration	explore	moon	universe
Since				

EXERCISE 2:   **Answer these questions in sentences.**

1.   Where is the Hubble Space Telescope?

____

2.   Why can the Hubble Space Telescope see things so clearly?

____

3.   How can we see things through the Hubble Space Telescope?

____

4.   How far away is the most distant thing the Hubble Space Telescope saw?

____

5.   How far is a light year?

____

6.   What was the problem with the Hubble Space Telescope for the first three years?

____

33

ACTIVITY 3:   **BINGO**

Before playing the game the students are to write the numbers of the words in LIST 1 beside the words with the same meaning in LIST 2.

LIST 1   **MATCH THE MEANING**

1 **cluster**	7 surprise	13 telescope	19 expensive
2 great deal	8 gradually	14 nebula	20 tank
3 light year	9 recently	15 solar system	21 to explore
4 advantage	10 mirror	16 universe	22 long range
5 distant	11astronomer	17 impact	23 terrible
6 ultra violet	12 to form	18 period	24 to increase

LIST 2   **WORDS TO CALL:**

far off   when one thing hits another
something unexpected   to make something
it costs a lot   a lot
a length of time space   to become larger
dust   not long ago

  1. group   a scientist who studies the stars
you carry liquids or gases in it   the sun and bodies orbiting it
stretching into the future   to travel for discovery
astronomers look through them   a kind of radiation from the sun
a bit at a time   benefit
you see yourself in it   everything in space
how far light travels in one year   very bad

		BINGO **FREE**		

EXERCISE 1:   Answer the questions true or false, by circling T or F in your book.
                    If you choose F, write in the correct answer.

1.   The space shuttle has three parts.

T | F ____

       ____
2.   The external fuel tank can be used again and again.

T | F ____

       ____
3.   The solid rocket boosters burn for nearly
        ten minutes.

T | F ____

       ____
4.   The crew rides in the solid rocket boosters.

T | F ____

       ____
5.   The space shuttle can carry people, equipment and
        tools into Earth orbit.

The Space Shuttle blasting off.
Photo courtesy of NASA.

T | F ____
6.   The orbiter can only be used once.

T | F ____
7.   The solid rocket boosters explode and burn up in the air.

T | F ____
8.   In two minutes the shuttle is nearly 100 kilometers in the air.

T | F ____
9.   The external fuel tank has a parachute for coming back to Earth.

T | F ____
10.   The orbiter burns up in the air.

T | F ____
11.   The shuttle can carry big loads in its cargo bay.

T | F ____

EXERCISE 2:   **Make good sentences of the words below.**

1.   that could They be over over built a spacecraft used and.

____

2.   in Earth The orbiter the returns to crew.

____

3.   sea the solid rocket fall boosters The into.

____

4.   carrying bay tools a equipment huge There cargo for and is.

____

5.   colored is huge fuel The tank rust external.

____

6.   Earth 45 shuttle minutes above the is over kilometers two In.

____

7.   on five crew usually flight to seven are members There each.

____

EXERCISE 3:   **Divide into groups of two or three. Make a conversation about the shuttle.**
Then role-play the conversation.

You: The two solid rocket boosters must be really powerful to lift the shuttle nearly fifty
kilometers into the air in just two minutes. Do you think the crew is uncomfortable?

Friend: ____

You: Yes, but even with good seats, they must feel something, going up that fast! Do you think
they get sick?

Friend: ____

You: Yes, they have a lot of training. I guess they get used to that much acceleration. Would
you like to go on a space shuttle mission?

Friend: ____

You: Yes, I'd like to go, too. It would be great to look down and see the earth below.

Friend: ____

Student Workbook

EXERCISE 1: Make good sentences out of the words below:

1.   lift engineers that tool things could a heavy The needed.

____

2.   ride the Astronauts on Canadarm sometimes.

____

3.   was company by The Canadian Canadarm made a robotics.

____

4.   Telescope they when the Canadarm used repaired the They Hubble.

____

5.   excited Canadarm were the about crew new The.

____

6.   of Canadarm use orbiters the the All.

____

7.   it up night stayed to They all test.

____

8.   Earth controllers goodnight to said their They on.

____

9.   arm was a very like strong It.

____

10.   inside orbiter is from It the controlled.

____

11.   equipment is heavy good for It moving.

____

12.   the in are joints Canadarm There six.

____

13.   Canadarm enjoyed crew using the The.

____

14.   better expected much worked than It they.

____

15.   is useful Canadarm a very tool The.

____

EXERCISE 2: CROSSWORD PUZZLE.

ACROSS

1 in place of
3 where your arm starts
5 things you work with
7 you have five on each hand
8 to finish
10 it lifts things
11 to fix
14 to make shorter
15 to like something
16 astronauts ride in it
18 they orbit the earth

DOWN

2 they go into space
4 means outside
6 a list of things to do at certain times
9 to try out
12 where an arm bends
13 design and use of robots
17 brown color

38

EXERCISE 1: Answer the questions in sentences.

1. Why didn't the Mars rovers crash when they landed on Mars?

   ____

2. The scientists thought the Mars rovers would stop working after 90 days. Did the Mars rovers keep going after 90 days?

   ____

3. What are the Mars rovers doing on Mars?

   ____

4. Did the space shuttle take the rovers to Mars?

   ____

5. Why don't the rovers run out of fuel?

   ____

6. Is Mars a dusty place?

   ____

7. Do scientists think that there could be some forms of life on Mars today?

   ____

8. Was Mars always a dry, dusty place?

   ____

9. Are there ever dust storms on Mars?

   ____

10. Are the rovers mobile?

    ____

EXERCISE 2: Fill in the blanks using the words below.

Mars has an _______________________ that is too hostile for people so the scientists sent

two _______________________ _______________________ called rovers to travel the surface of

the _______________________ . These rovers send back _______________________ of pictures

and a lot of _______________________ about Mars. They get _______________________ from the

sun, so they won't run out of _______________________ .

fuel	robots	information	thousands
mobile	atmosphere	planet	power

39

EXERCISE 3:

MATCH THE MEANING
Write the correct meaning beside the words, using the definitions seen below:

mobile ____

amazing ____

possibly ____

blow ____

to study ____

robot ____

controller ____

to change ____

storm ____

softly ____

opportunity ____

information ____

USE THESE WORDS:

to learn about something	bad weather	to make something different
a good chance	a programmable machine	what the wind does
facts about something somebody	it moves	gently
who directs something	around very	maybe
	surprising	

EXERCISE 1: Answer the questions in sentences.

1. How do the modules of the Space Station get into space?

   ____

2. Where does the power for the space station come from?

   ____

3. When did astronauts start living in the space station?

   ____

4. Why is the space station made of modules?

   ____

5. Is there any gravity in the space station?

   ____

6. What do the astronauts do in the space station?

   ____

7. Why do the solar panels on the space station turn?

   ____

8. Is there any atmosphere in space?

   ____

9. Where is the space station being built?

   ____

10. Do the astronauts use the Canadarm to help them build the space station?

   ____

Cosmonaut Salizhan Sharipov floats in the Zvezda Service Module.

Photo courtesy of NASA.

EXERCISE 2:

_______________the past times _______________ always looked into the_______________ . The

stars, the moon and the _______________ are so beautiful! "Wouldn't it be great if we could

_______________ through the air like the _______________!" he said.

_______________ thousands of flights in gliders, the Wright brothers built

the_______________ airplane. _______________people were flying _______________. People then

started to look at the. _______________ "We should go there _______________!" they said. So the

engineers, scientists and _______________ worked for years, and one day, a man

_______________on the moon. Today, people are in _______________ space at the Space Station.

Do you _______________that some day _______________will live on _______________planets?

USE THESE WORDS

too	pilots	After	In
first	moon	think	fly
other	birds	living	sky
mankind	planets	people	walked
everywhere	Soon		

EXERCISE 3:Make good sentences of the words below:

1.   is space panels its with station electricity that uses made solar The.

   ____

2.   space new module others into of the station fits Each the.

   ____

3.   the astronauts station live in space The.

   ____

4.   brought The shuttle there by the is space crew.

   ____

5.   many there are doing Scientists experiments.

   ____

EXERCISE 4: Crossword Puzzle:

ACROSS

4 right now
5 you clean your teeth with it
8 it grows in a garden
11 without stopping
14 very surprising
16 make something work
17 a programmable machine
18 the whole thing

DOWN

1 ill
2 to stay in the air
3 a tube for moving liquid or gas
6 a good chance
7 facts about something
9 a place for scientific research
10 part
12 push together
13 a part of a group
15 nothing or no

43

ANSWER THE QUESTIONS IN SENTENCES: (4 marks each)

1.	If you were hungry, would you go to a restaurant?

____

2.	Were the early planes used for reconnaissance?

____

3.	If you are tired, will you go to bed early?

____

4.	Is airplane flight dangerous today?

____

5.	If you went to London would you visit the queen?

____

6.	How could the astronauts breathe when they were on the surface of the moon?

____

7.	A lot of men flew into space. Are there women astronauts too?

____

Make good sentences of the words below: (4 marks each)

8.	to orbiter The work have outside astronauts the sometimes.

____

9.	are the orbiting you be hard sleep must when to earth It.

____

10.	Neil excited all the moon stepped world were Armstrong over onto when People the.

____

11.	there days is any in space, so no aren't There rainy atmosphere.

____

12.	want into go though people to is space Even it dangerous,.

____

44

Fill in the blanks, using the words below: (2 marks each)

Wilbur and Orville Wright worked very (13)_____________________, and they had

some difficult times. People didn't (14) _____________________ they could make a

(15) _____________________ that could fly. They made a number of small planes without

(16) _____________________. These planes are called (17) _____________________.

They couldn't find an engine that was (18) _____________________ enough for their planes.

(19) _____________________ they built their own engine. After a great deal of

(20) _____________________they were (21) _____________________. All their hard work

made them (22) _____________________.

USE THESE WORDS

successful	**believe**	**difficulty**	**famous**	**hard**
light	**gliders**	**finally**	**machine**	**engines**

MATCH THE MEANING (2 marks each)

23. astronauts _____________________ 24. disaster _____________________

25. cargo bay _____________________ 26. external _____________________

27. crane _____________________ 28. tiny _____________________

29. satellites _____________________ 30. tools _____________________

31. spacecraft _____________________ 32. stranded _____________________

33. hill _____________________ 34. famous _____________________

35. pilot _____________________ 36. wind _____________________

37. history _____________________ 38. to joke _____________________

Use the words given on the next page

45

USE THESE WORDS:

where the shuttle carries
things it makes the air move
very small
 everyone knows you
they go into space
means outside
 something very bad
he/she drives the plane

to be left behind where
the ground rises they
orbit Earth
it happened in the past
it lifts things
astronauts ride in it
things you work with
to say something funny

Photo courtesy of NASA.

46

ENGLISH	NOTES	ENGLISH	NOTES
accelerate, to (accelerated)		ceremony	
accept, to (accepted)		change, to (changed)	
accident		chase, to (chased)	
accomplish, to (accomplished)		Civil War	
ace		clean, to (cleaned)	
achievemnet		cluster	
advantage		Cold War	
agency		color	
aircraft		combat	
airline		Communism	
amazing		company	
anthem		competition	
area		complete, to (completed)	
arrange, to (arranged)		concern, to (concerned)	
astonishing		conditions	
astronomer		contain, to (contained)	
atmosphere		continuously	
attacker		contraption	
attempt, to (attempted)		control, to (controlled)	
automobile		controller	
aviator		cordage	
balloon		cover, to (covered)	
baron		crane	
battle		crash, to (crashed)	
battlefield		creature	
benefit		crew	
billion		crisis	
blast off		cylinder	
blow, to (blew)		damage, to (damaged)	
body		decide, to (decided)	
booster		defense	
born, to be (was born)		deliver, to (delivered)	
bravery		democratic	
break, to (broke)		demonstration	
breathe, to (breathed)		descend	
brush, to (brushed)		design, to (designed)	
build, to (built)		destination	
bush		destroy, to (destroyed)	
cabin		determine, to (determined)	
canon ball		develop, to (developed)	
capsule		die, to (died)	
cargo bay		dig, to (dug)	
carol		discover, to (discovered)	
carry, to (carried)		distant	

ENGLISH	NOTES	ENGLISH	NOTES
dragon		gas	
dusty		gather, to (gathered	
eagle		gentle	
earn, to (earned)		giant	
education		giraffe	
elbow		glare	
electric		glider	
elite		glimpse	
enemy		goal	
engine		goddess	
engineer		government	
enjoy, to (enjoyed)		gradually	
enormous		gravity	
entire		great deal	
equipment		grenade	
era		handle	
escape, to (escaped)		happen, to (happened)	
eventually		headquarters	
excited		heal, to (healed)	
expect, to (expected)		helicopter	
expensive		hero	
experiment		hide, to (hid)	
explode, to (exploded)		history	
explore, to (explored)		hop, to (hopped)	
external		hostile	
face plate		human body	
face, to (faced)		hydrogen	
failure		immediately	
faint		impact	
fall apart, to (fell apart)		imply, to (implied)	
fascinate, to (fascinated)		impressive	
feather		improve, to (improved)	
federation		increase, to (increased)	
finger		industry	
fireworks		information	
float, to (floated)		infra red	
flyer		instead	
footprint		international	
force		invention	
form, to (formed)		joint	
forth		joke, to (joked)	
fuel		journal	
fuel cell		jungle	
garden		kingdom	

ENGLISH	NOTES	ENGLISH	NOTES
kite		patent, to (patented)	
laboratory		period	
land, to (landed)		pilot	
launch, to (launched)		pipe	
leader		plan, to (planned)	
lift, to (lifted)		plant	
light year		platform	
living		point	
load		popular	
long range		possibly	
lucky		postage	
lunar		pour, to (poured)	
magnetic field		power	
material		praise, to (praised)	
maze		prediction	
melt, to (melted)		prison	
member		propeller	
message		provide, to (provided)	
microchip		push, to (pushed)	
military		push, to (pushed)	
mirror		puzzle	
mobile		radiation	
model		radio wave	
module		rank	
monkey		reaction	
motor		reassemble, to (reassembled)	
mutt		recently	
mythology		reconnaissance	
nebula		record, to (recorded)	
nephew		recruit, to (recruited)	
North Pole		refer, to (referred)	
nuclear bomb		reflection	
observation		religious	
ocean		remember, to (remembered)	
offer, to (offered)		repair, to (repaired)	
operate, to (operated)		reporter	
opportunity		return, to (returned)	
orbit, to (orbited)		revolution	
organize, to (organized)		ridiculous	
own, to (owned)		righteousness	
oxygen		risky	
page		robotics	
partridge		rocket	
passenger		rope	

ENGLISH	NOTES	ENGLISH	NOTES
rover		tent	
rust		terrible	
sample		test, to (tested)	
satellite		throne	
scary		tool	
scenario		toothpaste	
schedule		tower	
sea		track	
separate, to (separated)		transatlantic	
shine, to (shone)		transportation	
shorten, to (shortened)		travel	
shoulder		treaty	
sick		triplane	
signal		tube	
site		turtle	
snake		type	
softly		ultra violet	
solar panel		unable	
solar system		unfortunately	
solid rocket		unit	
space station		universe	
spacecraft		untrue	
spectacular		upright	
spin, to (spun)		upwards	
spirit		vacuum cleaner	
squeeze		victory	
stamp		wait, to (waited)	
steady, to (steadied)		wax	
storm		wealthy	
stranded		weapon	
strength		wind tunnel	
study, to (studied)		wing	
sub-orbital		withdraw, to (withdrew)	
success		wore	
super power		wrist	
surface		zero	
surprise			
survive, to (survived)			
symbol			
system			
taffeta			
tank			
teach, to (taught)			
telescope			

The History of Flight

Intermediate to Advanced ESL Lesson plans

Teacher Guide

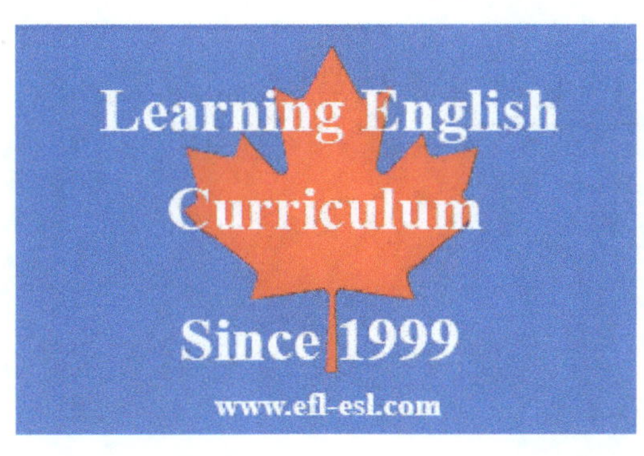

Lesson 1

ORAL QUESTIONS

Are people still fascinated with the sky?
Yes, they are still fascinated with the sky.

Who was Mercury said to be?
He was said to be messenger of the gods.

Why could he travel quickly?
He had wings on his feet and hat.

How did the emperor of Persia travel through the air?
He sat on his throne and eagles lifted him into the air.

Who had a symbol of a winged sun?
The ancient Egyptians had a symbol of a winged sun.

Who believed in Pegasus?
The Greeks believed in Pegasus.

Were there flying creatures in ancient mythology?
Yes, there were flying creatures in ancient mythology.

EXERCISE 1:

1. Why could Mercury travel very fast?
   He had wings on his feet and hat.
2. How could the emperor in Persia see all parts of his kingdom?He
   had eagles come and lift him into the air.
3. Does ancient mythology have stories about creatures that could fly?
   Yes, ancient mythology has stories about creatures that could fly
4. What was Pegasus?
   It was a flying horse.

EXERCISE 2: Crossword Puzzle solution.

<table>
<tr><td></td><td></td><td></td><td></td><td></td><td></td><td>S</td><td>N</td><td>A</td><td>K</td><td>E</td><td></td><td></td></tr>
<tr><td></td><td></td><td></td><td></td><td></td><td></td><td>Y</td><td></td><td></td><td></td><td>A</td><td></td><td></td></tr>
<tr><td>T</td><td></td><td></td><td></td><td>M</td><td></td><td>M</td><td></td><td>F</td><td></td><td>G</td><td></td><td></td></tr>
<tr><td>H</td><td></td><td></td><td></td><td>Y</td><td></td><td>B</td><td></td><td>A</td><td></td><td>L</td><td></td><td></td></tr>
<tr><td>R</td><td>I</td><td>G</td><td>H</td><td>T</td><td>E</td><td>O</td><td>U</td><td>S</td><td>N</td><td>E</td><td>S</td><td>S</td></tr>
<tr><td>O</td><td></td><td></td><td></td><td>H</td><td></td><td>L</td><td></td><td>C</td><td></td><td></td><td></td><td></td></tr>
<tr><td>N</td><td></td><td></td><td></td><td>O</td><td></td><td></td><td></td><td>I</td><td></td><td></td><td></td><td></td></tr>
<tr><td>E</td><td></td><td></td><td></td><td>L</td><td></td><td></td><td></td><td>N</td><td></td><td></td><td></td><td></td></tr>
<tr><td></td><td></td><td></td><td></td><td>O</td><td></td><td>D</td><td>R</td><td>A</td><td>G</td><td>O</td><td>N</td><td></td></tr>
<tr><td></td><td>W</td><td>I</td><td>N</td><td>G</td><td>S</td><td></td><td></td><td>T</td><td></td><td></td><td></td><td></td></tr>
<tr><td></td><td></td><td></td><td></td><td>Y</td><td></td><td></td><td>H</td><td>E</td><td>E</td><td>L</td><td></td><td></td></tr>
</table>

ORAL QUESTIONS

Where did Daedalus and Icarus live? — They lived in Greece.
What did they want to do? — They wanted to fly.
Why did they want to fly. — They wanted to escape from prison.
What did Daedalus make the wings from? — He made them from wax and feathers.

What did Daedalus tell Icarus before they flew? — He told him not to fly too high.
Did Icarus listen to his father? — No, he didn't listen to his father.
What happened to Icarus? — He flew too high and his wings melted. He fell into the sea.
How did Icarus die?
Who was Perdix? — Perdix was Daedalus' nephew.
Was Perdix smart? — Yes, Perdix was very smart.
What did Daedalus do to Perdix? — He pushed him off a high tower.
Did Perdix die from the fall? — No, he was changed into a partridge,
Who saved him? — The goddess Minerva saved him.

EXERCISE 1:

1. What did the king ask Daedalus to build?
   He asked him to build a maze.
2. What happened to Daedalus and Icarus after the maze was built? *They were put in prison.*
3. How did Daedalus and Icarus escape?
   Icarus made wings and they flew out.
4. What were the wings made of?
   They were made of feathers and wax.
5. Why did Icarus fall into the sea?
   He flew too close to the sun and his wings melted.
6. Why didn't Daedalus like Perdix?
   Perdix was smarter than him.
7. Why didn't Perdix die when he was pushed off the tower?
   Minerva changed him into a partridge.
8. Why do people say that partridges don't like to fly too high?
   They say that they still remember falling off the tower.

EXERCISE 2:

1. Daedalus very called who was was man smart a There.
   There was a man called Daedalus who was very smart.
2. fell melted sea wings, and The Icarus sun his into the.
   The sun melted his wings and Icarus fell into the sea.
3. father and high He to his flew listen very didn't.
   He didn't listen to his father and flew very high.
4. his and hat little wings that he had was on It said heels
   It was said that he had little wings on his hat and heels.
5. a Greeks Pegasus called had flying horse The even. *The Greeks even had a flying horse called Pegasus.*

6. himself, feathers wax made wings for using two and big He.
    He made two big wings for himself using wax and feathers.
7. pushed Daedalus a high day, Perdix tower One off.
    One day, Daedalus pusher Perdix off a high tower.

EXERCISE 3:

Daedalus and Icarus lived in **ancient** Greece. Daedalus worked for a **very rich** king.

This king asked Daedalus to make him a **beautiful** maze. He wanted it to be an

impossible place, so that no one could ever find their way out. When it was finished, Daedalus was

a **wise** man, because he was the **only** person who knew how to get out of the **terrible** maze. The

king didn't want Daedalus to tell **other** people, so he put him and his **young** son Icarus in prison.

Daedalus was **too** smart for the king. He made **huge** wings for himself and Icarus. One **sunny** day

the **happy** Daedalus and Icarus flew over the **high** walls.

Icarus flew too close to the **warm** sun. He fell into the **deep** ocean.

EXERCISE 4:

MATCH THE MEANING

myth	*stories from long ago*		partridg	*a bird*
garden	*a place of flowers and bushes*		e tower	*a very high building*
feather	*birds have them on their wings*		escape	*to get away*
throne	*a king or queen sits on it*		righteousness	*goodness*
dragon	*a mythical creature*			
maze	*a big puzzle*		nephew	*your sister's son*
			prison	*where they put bad people*

Lesson 3

ORAL QUESTIONS

Did Montgolfier gas make the balloons rise?	*No, it was hot air that made them rise.*
What happened to their first balloon?	*People destroyed it.*
What did they make their balloons of?	*They made them of thin wood and taffeta.*
Why did they send the sheep, duck and rooster up in the first flight?	*They didn't know if it would be safe for humans to fly in the balloon.*

On the flight before the king, did the balloon go up very high?

Yes, it went up about 500 meters.

Why did the brothers make the fire in the balloon very smoky?

They thought the smoke lifted the balloon.

Did the sheep, the duck and the rooster survive the flight?

Yes, they survived the flight.

Did many people see the first flight?

Yes, a huge crowd came to see it.

Did King Louis enjoy seeing the first flight?

No, he didn't enjoy it.

Why didn't he enjoy it?

He didn't like all the smoke.

EXERCISE 1:

1. What did the Montgolfier brothers build?
    They built a balloon.
2. What did they put in their first balloon?
    They put a duck, a sheep, and a rooster in the first balloon.
3. Did the duck, the sheep, and the rooster fly through the air?
    Yes, the duck, the sheep, and the rooster flew through the air.
4. What important people watched the two brothers on their first flight?
    The king and his wife watched the first flight.
5. Where did they get the hot air to make the balloon rise?
    They got the hot air from a fire.
6. What did the brothers think caused the balloon to rise?
    They thought the smoke caused it to rise.
7. Do you think their balloon flights were dangerous?
    Yes, I think they were dangerous.
8. The Montgolfier brothers went up in their balloon in 1783. Do people still go up in balloons?
    Yes, people still go up in balloons.

EXERCISE 2:   **Put the word in brackets ( ) into the correct tense.**

1. If I **had** a chicken, I would eat it.
2. I would ride my bicycle if I **had** it with me.
3. Maria would phone you tonight if she **were** at home.
4. You could see a movie if you **had** time.
5. If I **were** you, I wouldn't do that.
6. If you **were** rich would you be happy?
7. If I **were** king, you could be my queen.
8. If we **had** wings, we could fly.
9. If you **saw** her, you would like her.
10. He would be angry if he **were** here.
11. If I **had** the money, I would buy some coffee.

4

ACTIVITY 3:

BINGO

1	prison	where they put bad people a
2	tower	very high building
3	righteousness	goodness
4	myth	stories from long ago
		a big puzzle
5	maze	birds have them on their wings
6	feather	
7	partridge	a bird
8	dragon	a mythical creature
9	nephew	your brother's son
10	garden	a place of flowers and bushes
11	throne	a king or queen sits on it
12	escape	to get away
13	fascinate	to interest
14	snake	a long thin creature the
15	heel	back of your foot
16	ancient	very old
17	symbol	it stands for something else
18	kingdom	where the king rules
19	beautiful	very pretty
20	messenger	he carries messages
21	mind	you think with it
22	to heal	to make better
23	shine	what the sun does
24	to fly	to move through the air

Lesson 4

ORAL QUESTIONS

Would you be happy if you were a hero?

Yes, I'd be happy if I were a hero.
No, I wouldn't be happy if I were a hero.

Where would you live if you had a lot of money?

I'd live in ________ if I had a lot of money.

Would you fly in a balloon if you could?

Yes, I'd fly in a balloon if I could.
No, I wouldn't fly in a balloon if I could.

If you had time would you travel.

Yes, I'd travel if I had time.
No, I wouldn't travel if I had time.

If you were hungry would you go to a restaurant?

Yes, if I were hungry, I'd go to a restaurant.
No, if I were hungry, I wouldn't go to a restaurant.

If you had an apple would you eat it?

Yes, if I had an apple I'd eat it.
No, if I had an apple I wouldn't eat it.

Would you visit your friends if they were sick?

Yes, I'd visit my friends if they were sick.
No, I wouldn't visit my friends if they were sick. Yes, if I'm tired I'll go to bed early.

If you are tired will you go to bed early?

No, if I'm tired I won't go to bed early.

If you had a horse would you ride it?

Yes, if I had a horse I'd ride it.
No, if I had a horse I wouldn't ride it.

Will you have a holiday this summer if you have time?

Yes, I'll have a holiday if I have time. No, I won't have a holiday if I have time.

ACTIVITY 2: *POSSIBLE ANSWERS.*

You: I just read about the first people who really did fly through the air. It wasn't Daedalus and Icarus.

Your friend: *Who was it?*

You: It was the Montgolfier brothers in France. They did it for King Louis XVI and his wife Josephine.

Your friend: *How did they do it? Did they make wings?*

You: No, they didn't make wings, they made a balloon. They lit a fire under the balloon and it rose into the air. They thought it was the smoke that caused the balloon to rise, so they made a very smoky fire.

Your friend: *Was it their first balloon?*

You: No, it wasn't their first balloon, a couple of months before they put a sheep, a duck and a rooster in a balloon and made it fly.

Your friend: *Did the king like it?*

You: No, the king didn't enjoy it. The book says that the wind blew the smoke in the king's face, and he was not at all happy about it.

EXERCISE 1: Answer in sentences.

1. When were the Chinese people making kites?
   They were making them 2000 years ago.
2. Was Leonardo da Vinci interested in flying?
   Yes, he was interested in flying.
3. Did George Caley fly in his gliders?
   No, his gliders were only small models.
4. Did Caley fly a model with a small engine? *Yes, he flew a model with a small engine.*
5. Did Otto Lilienthal make many flights?
   Yes, he made more than 2500 flights.
6. Did Lilienthal have a motor in his planes? *No, his planes were all gliders.*
7. Were Lilienthal's flights dangerous?
   Yes, they were dangerous.
8. Why did Lilienthal stop flying?
   He was killed when one of his gliders crashed.

EXERCISE 2:
Crossword Puzzle solution:

ORAL QUESTIONS

If there were Zeppelins today would you
fly across the Atlantic in one?
Would you like to fly a kite?

Yes, I'd fly across the Atlantic in
one. Yes, I'd like to fly a kite.
No, I wouldn't like to fly a kite.

The first people to fly used gliders, didn't they?
Yes, they did.

Was Leonardo da Vinci interested in flying?
Yes, he was interested in flying.

What did Otto Lilienthal do?
He made many flights with
gliders. He died in a crash.

What happened to him?

When was the first flight with a motor?
It was in 1884.

What kind of flying machine made the
first flight?
It was a balloon with an electric motor.

Where did it fly?
It flew around the Eiffel Tower in Paris.

Do we see Zeppelins flying today?
Yes, we sometimes see Zeppelins flying today.
No, we don't see them flying today.

Would you fly to another country if you
had the money?

Yes, I'd fly to another country if I had the money.
No, I wouldn't fly to another country if I
had the money.

EXERCISE 1:

1. the, time, will, to, have, go, if, I, I, library
    I will go to the library if I have time.
2. phone, am, you, late, will, If, I, I
    If I am late I will phone you.
3. London, money, I, had, I, fly, enough, if, would, to
    I would fly to London if I had enough money.
4. I, I, if, him, would, him, tell, saw
    I would tell him if I saw him
5. see, ask, will, her, I, if, I, her
    I will ask her if I see her.
6. were, He, if, wouldn't, alone, there, he, go
    He wouldn't go there if he were alone.
7. early, car, I, I, the, If, home, wash, get, could
    If I get home early I could wash the car.
8. high, If, I, wouldn't, were, so, Icarus, I, fly
    If I were Icarus I wouldn't fly so high.
9. if, at, I, weren't, would, work, visit, she, her
    I would visit her if she weren't at work.
10. question, it, the, isn't, This, last, is?
    This is the last question, isn't it?

Activity 2 Student Reader:
Scenario 1: Suggest to the group what a new thing flying must have been.
Scenario 2: Suggest that it would be wonderful for people who get sea sick in boats.
Scenario 3: Suggest that it would likely be safer to go by boat, but the Zeppelin would be exciting.
Scenario 4: Point out that although it would be very exciting, it might also be very dangerous.

EXERCISE 2:

1.   Were Zeppelins the first flying machines to carry passengers?Yes,
      Zeppelins were the first flying machines to carry passengers.
2.   Who had the first patent on Zeppelins?
      Count von Zeppelin had the first patent.
3.   Did Zeppelins ever carry passengers across the Atlantic Ocean?
      Yes, they carried many passengers across the Atlantic Ocean.
4.   Were Zeppelins used during the First World War?
      Yes, Zeppelins were used during the First World War.
5.   Who started the first airline company in the world?
      Count von Zeppelin started the first airline company.

EXERCISE 3:

MATCH THE MEANING

wealthy	have a lot of money	transatlantic	crosses the Atlantic ocean
scenario	possible situation	reconnaissance	exploration for information
enemy	person or people against you	airline	a company that has airplanes
destination	where you are going	enormous	very large
accident	something bad that happens	to attempt	to try
glider	a plane with no motor	hydrogen	a very light gas

Lesson 6

ORAL QUESTIONS

Where did the Wright brothers work?
Did they have many difficulties building
the first plane?
On their first flight, did they fly very far?
Do you think their early flights were dangerous?

Even though the first flights were dangerous
the Wright brothers kept trying, didn't they?
Orville and Wilbur Wright weren't engineers,
were they?
Many people fly today, don't they?
Airplane travel is much faster than land
travel, isn't it?

Did the Wright brothers ever fly in gliders?
Has airplane flight made it easier to do
business in other countries?

They worked in a bicycle shop.

Yes, they had many difficulties.
No, they didn't fly very far.

Yes, I think they were dangerous.

Yes, they did. / Yes, they kept trying.

No, they weren't.
Yes, they do.

Yes, it is.

Yes, they flew many times in gliders.

Yes, it has made it easier to do business in
other countries.

Is airplane flight dangerous today?

Yes it is dangerous. / No, it isn't dangerous.

Why did the Wright brothers have to make their own gas engine?

The gas engines that they could buy then were too heavy for their airplane to lift.

I think the Wright brothers were very smart, don't you?

Yes, I think they were very smart.

ACTIVITY 3: POSSIBLE ANSWERS.

You: I read somewhere that the Wright Brothers were thinking of making a car before they got interested in flying.

Your Friend: Why didn't they do it?

You: Because they thought that people wouldn't want to buy a car.

Your Friend: They were wrong about that!

You: Yes, they really were wrong about that. If they had worked on a car, do you think that other people would have made an airplane?

Your Friend: Yes, a lot of people were interested in flight at the time.

You: Yes, I guess so. Do you know that very few people knew about their first flight?

Your Friend: Weren't there reporters from the newspapers there?

You: No, there were no reporters from the newspapers. There was one man that saw it all, though. His name was Amos Root. He had a journal for bee keepers called "Gleanings in Bee Culture". He wrote: "…these two brothers have probably not even a faint glimpse of what their discovery is going to bring to the children of men." He was right! No one knew what uses the airplane would have in the future.

Your Friend: It certainly changed transportation!

You: It used to take a long time to cross the ocean in a ship.

Your Friend:
You: Now it could be done in hours. It was good for business. Yes, it has changed international business a lot.

Your Friend:
You: It changed a lot of things, even though people thought it couldn't be done. The New York Times newspaper said that maybe in one million to ten million years people might be able to make a plane that would fly. Eight days later they did fly their plane! They fooled them, didn't they?

EXERCISE 1:

1.   How do you think Orville and Wilbur felt when their plane took off?
     I think they felt happy and excited.
2.   Their first flight at Kitty Hawk broke the wing of their plane. Why do you think they kept trying?
     They kept trying because they knew they could do it.

3.   Do you think their work with early airplanes was dangerous?
     Yes, I think it was dangerous.
4.   They read all of Otto Lilienthal's books on gliders. Do you think that this helped them?Yes,
     I think it helped them a lot.
5.   They must have been very smart, don't you think?
     Yes, I think they were very smart.
6.   Has air transportation changed what kind of food we eat?
     Yes, because food can be flown in from different parts of the world.
7.   Do a lot of people use airplanes for traveling on business?
     Yes, a lot of people use airplanes to travel on business.
8.   Why did they have to build their own engine for their first plane?
     They couldn't find an engine that was light enough.
9.   The New York Times newspaper said that they didn't think people would be able to make a
     plane that would fly. Why do you think they said that?
     They didn't think it was possible to build a plane that would fly.
10. Would you like to fly in one of the early planes?
     Yes, I'd like to fly in one of the early planes.
     No, I wouldn't like to fly in one of the early planes.

EXERCISE 2:

The brothers worked very hard and had some *difficult* times. It was December 17th 1903,

an historic day. They put the track on some *flat* ground and used the wind to *move*

the plane along it. Orville was the *pilot* while Wilbur ran beside it to steady the *wing* The

plane lifted off the *ground* for 12 seconds and flew for 120 feet. It was one of the great

events of the century.

ACTIVITY 4: DEBATE.

It isn't necessary to have an education to do well in life.

Here are some topics the students might think about:

PRO	**CON**
The Wright brothers did well without an education.	You need to have knowledge to get along in the world.
Many of our political leaders have not had an education.	All of the top engineers in the flight industry are highly educated.
People who think clearly can often do better than highly educated people.	In business you need an education to be able to run the office computer programs.
Most highly paid hockey players aren't highly educated.	Most unemployed people are uneducated.

ORAL QUESTIONS

When was the first military plane ordered? — It was ordered in 1909

What was it to be used for — It was to be used for reconnaissance.

How many seats did the first military plane have? — It had two seats.

Were Zeppelins used in the First War? — Yes, they were used in the First War.

Were enemy pilots friendly with each other at first? — Yes, they were friendly with each other at first.

Later the pilots carried rocks with them. What were the rocks for? — They threw them at enemy pilots.

Did soldiers on the ground shoot at enemy planes? — Yes, they shot at enemy planes.

Did airplanes become very useful weapons of war? — Yes, they became very useful weapons of war.

EXERCISE 1:

The first *military* planes were used for *reconnaissance* . When the pilots saw other pilots, they *waved* to them. Soon, the pilots starting throwing things at the other pilots. Then they *decided* that the planes could be a very good way to kill the *enemy* . They put heavy *machine guns* in the planes, so they could shoot down the enemy planes. Often a plane would chase another plane for a long time, trying to get close enough to *shoot* the other one down. It was like a very *dangerous* game they were playing, and if you lost, you *died*.
Some pilots shot down many planes before they were *finally* killed.

EXERCISE 2:

1. What were the first military planes used for?
   They were used for reconnaissance.
2. Did the soldiers on the ground sometimes shoot at the enemy planes?
   Yes, they often shot at the enemy planes.
3. Were the first pilots friendly to the enemy pilots?
   Yes, they were friendly to them at first.
4. Were many of the pilots killed in the war?
   Yes, many pilots were killed.
5. Did the military use Zeppelins during the first war?
   Yes, they used Zeppelins.
6. Do you think the Wright brothers thought that airplanes would be used in warfare when they started to build their first airplane?
   No, I don't think they thought they would be used for warfare.

EXERCISE 3:   **MATCH THE MEANING**

unfortunately	unluckily	military	to do with the armed forces
prediction	to tell about the future	risky	dangerous
invention	the making of something new	aircraft	a flying vehicle
grenade	a bomb that is thrown	weapon	something you fight with
eventually	finally	hero	a very brave person
bravery	not being afraid	observation	looking at something carefully

EXERCISE 4:

1.   The New York Times didn't think it was possible for people to fly.
     Wilbur and Orville Wright made an airplane.
     The New York Times didn't think it was possible for people to fly, but Wilbur and Orville made an airplane anyway.
2.   There were many disappointments.
     The brothers kept working.
     Although / Even though there were many disappointments the brothers kept working.
3.   The Wright brothers thought about building an automobile.
     They decided that no one would want to buy one.
     The Wright brothers thought about building an automobile, but they decided that no one would want to buy one.
4.   They needed to study different wing shapes.
     They built a wind tunnel.
     They needed to study different wing shapes so they built a wind tunnel.
5.   Their model planes kept crashing in the wind tunnel.
     They kept making new ones.
     Their model planes kept crashing in the wind tunnel but they kept making new ones.
6.   No one thought that people could ever fly.
     Orville and Wilbur fooled them.
     Even though / Although no one thought that people could ever fly, Orville and Wilbur fooled them.
7.   Orville and Wilbur were very peaceful people.
     The military turned their invention into a weapon of war.
     Orville and Wilbur were very peaceful people but the military turned their invention into a weapon of war anyway.
8.   Flying an airplane in the war was very dangerous.
     Lots of young men wanted to do it.
     Flying an airplane in the war was very dangerous, but lots of young men wanted to do it anyway.
9.   The Wright brothers couldn't find a gas engine light enough to drive an airplane.
     They had to build their own engine.
     The Wright brothers couldn't find a gas engine light enough to drive an airplane so they had to build their own engine.
10. Some planes were shot down by soldiers on the ground.
     The greatest risk was being shot down by other pilots.
     Some planes were shot down by soldiers on the ground but the greatest risk was being shot down by other pilots.

Lesson 8

ORAL QUESTIONS

What were the first military planes used for? — They were used for reconnaissance.

Why were the planes good for reconnaissance? — The pilots could see the enemy's forces and see what they were planning.

Why was it dangerous to fly a military plane? — The planes were fragile and could be shot down. Who shot down the most planes in World War I? — The Red Baron shot down the most planes. What was the name of the Red Baron's elite flying group? — It was called the Red Baron's Flying Circus.

Why did the Red Baron make a list of rules for his group? — He wanted them to be the best pilots.

Why did the Red Baron have a red plane? — He wanted his other pilots to be able to see him.

Why did this make his job much more dangerous? — This made it easier for the enemy to see him.

When was the Red Baron finally shot down? — He was shot down in 1918.

EXERCISE 1: *POSSIBLE ANSWERS.*

Your Friend: I read that what Captain Dickenson said was true, when he made a prediction about warfare in the air.

YOU: He was the first military man to fly, wasn't he?

Your Friend: Yes, he said that at first the first planes would be used for reconnaissance. From the air, you could see where the enemy was, and what they were doing, but later, there would be fighting in the air.

YOU: What happened when both sides had planes in the air?

Your Friend: That's very interesting. The planes were open, and it was very easy for the pilots to see each other. So, as the planes passed each other, the pilots would wave.

YOU: That's very strange! These pilots were enemies!

Your Friend: It is strange, isn't it? Later, they started to carry rocks and even grenades in their planes, so they could throw them at the other pilots. Finally, like Captain Dickenson predicted, they carried guns with them.

YOU: Did the pilots shoot other planes down?

Your Friend: Yes. Some of the pilots became very good at it. They also had the soldiers on the ground shooting at them. A number of the first pilots became great heroes because of their bravery. It was very dangerous, and quite a few men were killed.

EXERCISE 2:

1. What was the Red Baron's elite flying group called?
   It was called the Red Baron's Flying Circus.
2. Flying over enemy lines was very risky, wasn't it?
   Yes, it was very risky.
3. Do you think the Red Baron was a very good pilot, or was he just lucky?
   I think he was a good pilot. / I think he was just lucky.
4. Do you think the Red Baron was happy about his success, or do you think he worried about all the men he killed?
   I think he was happy with his success.

13

EXERCISE 3: CROSSWORD PUZZLE.

Crossword answers:

- HEADQUARTERS
- FLYER
- CHASE
- COMBAT
- BATTLEFIELD
- DETERMINED
- ACCEPT
- UNIT
- TRIP PLANE
- ACE
- EARN
- ELITE
- EVENTUALLY
- EQUIPMENT

ACTIVITY 3 STUDENT READER

Scenario 1: Suggest the moral issue of killing the other pilots.

Scenario 2: Point out to this group how dangerous the little planes were and how safe air travel is today.

Scenario 3: A few suggested names might be helpful: Louis Pasteur, Madame Curie, Thomas Edison, Albert Einstein.

Lesson 9

ORAL QUESTIONS

Who made the first rockets?	The Chinese made the first rockets.
Why did the armies stop using rockets in warfare?	They stopped using rockets because the new canons were better.
When did they start using rockets again in warfare?	They started using rockets again in the Second World War.
How did the Germans use rockets?	They used rockets to bomb the cities in England.
Did the rockets kill many people?	Yes, they killed many people.
Why were people afraid of the rockets?	They were afraid because they could carry nuclear bombs.
What happened on October 4th 1957?	The Russians launched Sputnik I.
Why were the Americans surprised?	They thought that they would be the first to launch a satellite.
What did Sputnik II carry into space?	It carried a dog into space.
Do you think the Russians should have used dogs in their space program?	Yes, I think they should have used dogs. No, I don't think they should have used dogs.

EXERCISE 1:

1. to Chinese People rockets the were the first use that think. People think that the Chinese were the first to use rockets.
2. 1000 AD before were using They likely rockets. They likely were using rockets before 1000 AD.
3. rockets the Boulogne with destroyed French The town of British. The British destroyed the French town of Boulogne with rockets.

14

4. Sputnik I to used The powerful launch Russians a rocket.
    The Russians used a powerful rocket to launch Sputnik I.
5. start Age launch of of Sputnik I Space was the the The.
    The launch of Sputnik I was the start of the Space Age.
6. do things that showed the Soviets they could The world great.
    The Soviets showed the world that they could do great things.
7. no afraid Even people carried weapons, it though made Sputnik.
    Even though Sputnik carried no weapons, it made people afraid.
8. to up The to work hard Americans had catch.
    The Americans had to work hard to catch up.
9. Earth it sent radio orbited waves as Sputnik back.
    Sputnik sent radio waves back as it orbited Earth.

EXERCISE 2:

We think that rockets were ***developed*** in China more than three thousand years ***ago.***

They were used a lot by ***military*** forces to start fires. They ***always*** scared people, too. During

World War 2, Hitler had scientists work on ***rockets*** for a long time. They made several kinds of

rockets that they sent to England with ***bombs*** in them. These rockets killed a lot of people.

Then, in 1957, the USSR ***surprised*** the world. It launched Sputnik. This was a very

small ***satellite***, but it circled the earth every 98 minutes and sent radio messages back to Earth.

ACTIVITY 3:

MATCH THE MEANING

1	chase	*to go after and try to catch*	13	glare	*something very bright*
2	accept	*to take something given a*	14	satellite	*it orbits the earth*
3	unit	*person, thing, or group*	15	launch	*to send off*
4	finally	*eventually*	16	canon ball	*it comes from a canon*
5	earn	*to get something by working for it*	17	nuclear bomb	*a very dangerous bomb*
6	elite	*someone very good at something*	18	to orbit	*to circle*
7	headquarters	*the main office*	19	anthem	*a kind of song*
8	combat	*fighting*	20	radio wave	*it comes from a radio*
9	aviator	*flyer*	21	to develop	*to change and grow or improve*
10	battlefield	*where combat takes place*	22	accomplish	*to finish*
11	triplane	*a plane with three wings*	23	weapon	*something to fight with*
12	ace	*the very best*	24	risky	*dangerous*

15

ORAL QUESTIONS

Why did they call it the "Space Race"? United States and the Soviet Union were in a race to show the world which country was best.

Which country put the first satellite into orbit? The Soviet Union put the first satellite into orbit. Where did Laika come from? Laika came from the streets of Moscow.

Why was the world surprised when the Soviets launched Sputnik I? No one knew that they were able to do it at that time.

Why were people afraid when the Soviets launched Sputnik I? It meant that the Soviets could carry nuclear bombs in their rockets.

Did Sputnik I carry any bombs? No, it didn't carry any bombs.

Why did many German rocket scientists leave Germany after the war? They were offered good jobs in the USA and the USSR.

Did the research for the space race help people in other ways? Yes, it helped people in other ways.

Do people use satellites today? Yes, they use them for many things.

Did the countries learn a lot about rockets as a result of the space race? Yes, they learned a lot about rockets.

Would the Internet work without satellites? No, it wouldn't work without satellites.

EXERCISE 1:

Possible answers that "You" would say:

Friend: We have come a long way since the first flight by the Wright brothers, haven't we?
You: ***Yes, we have. Things have changed a lot.***
Friend: People fly all around the world, in fast planes, and aren't the rockets of today different?
You: ***The scientists have learned a lot about rockets.***
Friend: Poor Laika! It must have been a terrible trip in Sputnik II!
You: ***She didn't have a good life on the streets.***

Friend: Do you think Laika would have been able to live through the winter on the streets of Moscow?
You: ***No, it gets very cold there.***
Friend: When Sputnik II ran out of air, Laika probably just went to sleep and then died in her sleep. That wasn't too bad.
You: ***Maybe that was better than freezing to death in Moscow.***

EXERCISE 2:   **Answer the questions in sentences.**

1. Was the United States the first country to put a satellite into orbit?
    No, the Soviet Union was the first country to put a satellite into orbit.
2. Did Laika go in the first satellite?
    No, Laika went in the second satellite.

16

3.   Why did they send a dog into space?
      They wanted to be sure that a living creature could live through the blast off.
4.   Why did Khrushchev want the second satellite launched so soon after the first?
      He wanted to show the world what his country could do on the fortieth anniversary of the
      Bolshevik revolution.
5.   Did the Soviets have other dogs in their space program?
      Yes, they had many dogs in their space program.
6.   What happened to the dog called Bold?
      It ran away the night before it was to go into space.

EXERCISE 3:

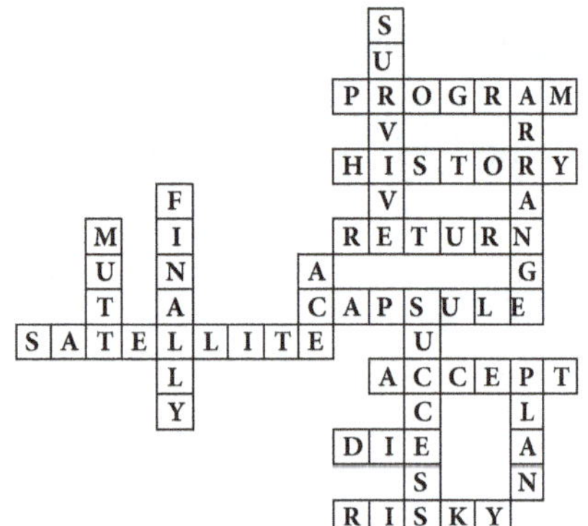

ACTIVITY 3 STUDENT READER:

Scenario 1: Suggest that there are animal rights groups all over the world trying to stop cruel experimentation.

Scenario 2: Point out to the group that the Soviet leader in charge of the rocket program later said that he was sorry he had used Laika.

Scenario 3: Suggest that there are millions of people who don't have clean water to drink, and they don't likely care about space exploration.

Scenario 4: Suggest that a good answer might be complete cooperation between the countries in space exploration.

Lesson 11

ORAL QUESTIONS

How did people feel when the USSR
launched Sputnik I?

They felt afraid.

Were the Americans very far behind in
the space race?

No, they weren't very far behind.

What was the goal of the space race?

The goal was to be the first to put someone on
the moon.

Why did each of the countries want to
win the race?

They wanted to show the world that they were
the best.

Was space flight dangerous?

Yes, it was very dangerous.

Did Sputnik I carry any weapons?

No, it didn't carry any weapons.

Did the Soviet Union and the United States work
together to learn about space?

No, they didn't work together.

Why did the military leaders of both countries
want to learn about space?

The military leaders of both countries wanted to
be able to put weapons in space.

EXERCISE 1:   **Possible answers that "Friend" would say:**

You: The Space Race changed the world forever, didn't it?
Friend: **Yes, it was a time of great change.**
You: At first it was like a war, without killing people. The Soviet Union wanted to show the world that they were the best, and that the Communist system was best for the people, and produced the best scientists. The Americans wanted to show the Soviets that they were the best. Because of the space race, amazing things were done.
Friend: **The scientists did a lot of research, didn't they? OR What were some of the things that were   done?**
You: During the space race, the scientists learned how to put a satellite in orbit. Without the satellites, you wouldn't be able to watch many of the television shows, and your cell phone wouldn't work.
Friend: **Now we can get hundreds of channels on our television sets. Do cell phones use satellites?**
You: Yes, most countries are using satellites for their telephone systems, as well as for cell phones. Without satellites, the Internet couldn't exist.
Friend: **Before the space race, computers were huge, but research changed all that.**
You: Because vehicles for space needed to be small and light, computers were changed to meet this need. Now, almost everything you use at home has a tiny microchip inside it to control how it works. This came from Space Race research.

EXERCISE 2:
During the Space Race the scientists learned to make everything small and light, so that they could carry their equipment in the spacecraft. We now have tiny chips in many of our household appliances. Can you name ten things that you find in most households that contain chips? (HINT: Often the chips are in the clocks.) Write the answers below:

1.	VCR	2.	television set
3.	coffee maker	4.	computers
5.	alarm clocks	6.	CD player
7.	I pod	8.	printer
9.	fax machine	10.	electric stove

EXERCISE 3:

MATCH THE MEANING

leaders	people follow them to	revolution	a fight to change government
prediction	tell about the future to	offer	to give someone a chance
to joke	say something funny a	brilliant	very smart
era	time in history	hostile	very unfriendly
competition	one side tries to beat the other	to return	to go back
bravery	not being afraid	blast off	when a rocket takes off

18

ACTIVITY 4:   PRO

They could have accomplished more for the same money.
It would have eased world tensions.
Both countries would have had economic benefits.

CON

Each was trying to prove that it was the best.
 It would have been too difficult because of the politics. Both sides would have had trouble cooperating.

Lesson 12

Why did the scientists send animals into space?

They wanted to see if living creatures could survive the dangers of rocket flight.

Who was the first man to orbit the earth?

Yuri Gagarin was the first man to orbit the earth.

Was he from the U.S.A.?

No, he was from the U.S.S.R.

Who was the first American to make a sub orbital flight?

Alan Shepard made the first sub-orbital flight.

Who was the first American to orbit the earth?

John Glenn was the first American to orbit the earth

Where did the capsule carrying John Glenn land? It landed in the ocean.

Where does a satellite in earth orbit go? It circles the earth.

How many times did John Glenn circle the earth?

He circled the earth three times.

Was manned rocket flight dangerous?

Yes, manned rocket flight was dangerous. Yes, I'd like to ride in a rocket.

Would you like to ride in a rocket?

No, I wouldn't like to ride in a rocket.

EXERCISE 1:

1. Both countries spent huge amounts of money on the Space Race. Do you think it was a good idea to spend the money that way? (Give the reasons for your answer.)
    Yes, I think it was a good idea to spend that money on space exploration because it helps us to understand our own world.
    No, I don't think it was a good idea to spend that money on space exploration because there are so many poor countries that could have been helped with that money.
2. What were the governments really interested in with their space programs?
    They were interested in the military use of space.
3. Both the USA and the Soviet Union were sending spacecraft into orbit. Why do you think they didn't work together?
    Both countries wanted to show the world that they were the best.
4. Both countries wanted to show the world that they were the best. Do you think putting an astronaut on the moon was a suitable way to prove that they were the best?
    Putting an astronaut on the moon was a very difficult task, so being able to do that would prove that they had very good scientists.
5. Do you think that someday people will live on other planets?
    Yes, I think that some day people will live on other planets.
    No, I don't think that people will ever live on other planets.

19

EXERCISE 2:

1. up, Soviet, was, but, the, Union, Americans, ahead, The, caught. The
    Soviet Union was ahead, but the Americans caught up.
2. times, earth, around, Shepard, flew, the, three, Alan.
    Alan Shepard flew three times around the earth.
3. the, Yuri, in, a, great, Union, hero, Soviet, became, Gagarin.
    Yuri Gagarin became a great hero in the Soviet Union.
4. many, for, Space, brought, Research, Race, benefits, the.
    Research for the Space Race brought many benefits.
5. war, for, use, The, space, wanted, leaders, weapons, to, military, of.
    The military leaders wanted to use space for weapons of war.
6. accidents, there, dangerous, many, flights, were, because, were, Space.
    Space flight was dangerous because there were many accidents.
7. a, Could, such, rocket, living, survive, flight, creatures?
    Could living creatures survive such a rocket flight?

ACTIVITY 3:   **BINGO**
LIST 1   **MATCH THE MEANING**

1	leaders	people follow them	13	program	a plan for doing things
2	revolution	a fight to change government	14	history	what has happened
3	prediction	to tell about the future	15	success	you get what you worked for
4	offer	to give someone a chance	16	survive	to stay alive to
5	to joke	to say something funny	17	to die	stop living
6	brilliant	smart	18	finally	eventually
7	era	time	19	satellite	it goes around the earth
8	hostile	very unfriendly	20	to accept	to take something that is given
9	competition	one side tries to beat the other	21	capsule	what the astronauts travel in
10	to return	to go back	22	dangerous	risky
11	bravery	not being afraid	23	prepare	to get things ready
12	blast off	when a rocket takes off	24	ace	someone very good at something

Lesson 13

ORAL QUESTIONS

What did Neil Armstrong mean when
he said "a giant leap for mankind"?   He meant that people had accomplished a lot.

Why was the Apollo program popular
in the United States?   It provided a lot of good jobs.

Did the USSR land a person on the moon?   No, they didn't land a person on the moon.

Did you follow in your father's footsteps? Yes, I followed in my father's footsteps.
                                           No, I didn't follow in my father's footsteps.

What is the surface of the moon called?   It is called the lunar surface.

Did some spacecraft crash into the lunar surface? Yes, some spacecraft crashed there.

20

Were the spacecraft that crashed
manned or unmanned? | They were unmanned.

While these spacecraft were descending to the
lunar surface, what were they doing? | They were taking pictures and sending them back to Earth.

How could the astronauts breathe when they
were on the surface of the moon? | They had air inside their spacesuits.

Are there wild animals living on the moon? | No, there are no wild animals living on the moon.

What did they bring back from the moon? | They brought back rock samples.

EXERCISE 1:   **Complete the sentences with the correct tense of "get".**

1.   The astronauts *got* busy learning how to walk in a space suit.
2.   The astronauts thought that they *would get* hungry if they didn't
3.   s*pace*craft *got/ was getting* ready to blast off.
4.   They *got/ were getting* safely back to earth after their long flight.
5.   Some companies *got/ were getting* rich building space craft.
6.   Armstrong had a bag of rocks that *got/ was getting* heavy.
7.   The astronauts *got/ were getting* sleepy traveling back to Earth.
8.   It was *got/ was getting* cloudy before they left.
9.   Their families were *getting* worried when they were returning.
10.   The engineers were *getting* happier by the minute.

EXERCISE 2: Answer the questions in sentences:

1.   Why was the Apollo Program popular in the United States?
        It provided many good jobs.
2.   Did the USSR continue with the race to the moon?
        No, it didn't continue the race.
3.   Why did Armstrong say it was a "giant leap for mankind"?
        Because landing on the moon was a great achievement.
4.   Did some unmanned flights crash on the lunar surface?
        Yes, some flights crashed on the lunar surface.
5.   What did the astronauts collect on the moon?
        They collected rock samples

EXERCISE 3: Possible answers.

Friend: That must have been pretty scary. I'd be too frightened to go to the moon. The
You: astronauts had a lot of training. I don't think they found it scary.
Friend: Maybe we would run out of fuel, or maybe the spacecraft would break down and
               leave me stranded on the moon.
You: That's ridiculous! The spacecraft never ran out of fuel.
Friend: No, it's not ridiculous! How do they know how much fuel it would take to go to the
               moon?

21

You:	*They can tell that before the spacecraft takes off.*
Friend:	Well, there are all kinds of other risks. I wouldn't like it at all!
You:	*The people at NASA studied the moon a lot before people went there.*
Friend:	I know that NASA sent lots of unmanned missions to study the moon, but it could be very different for people walking around on the moon.
You:	*I think the astronauts knew what to expect.*
Friend:	There's no air up there on the moon. Wouldn't it be awful if we went to the moon and there wasn't enough oxygen for us to breathe?
You:	*Yes, it would be terrible, but they knew how much oxygen to take.*
Friend:	What if the rockets didn't work properly? You really can't be sure. Then when you wanted to come home, the capsule might land at the North Pole, or in the jungle of Africa, or somewhere awful.
You:	*But they didn't! You just worry too much!*
Friend:	Yes, I guess you're right! I just like to stay at home.
You:	*Not everyone wants to be an astronaut.*

ACTIVITY 2: Hints for the students.

Scenario 1:

This group could think of using words like exciting, proud, fearful or heroic. Some in the group might be fearful, or anxious.

Scenario 2:

The families would certainly be proud and happy. The group might also use words like concerned, worried or anxious.

Scenario 3:

The scientists might think about some of the worries they had before the mission, and how hard they had to work to overcome the obstacles.

EXERCISE 4:

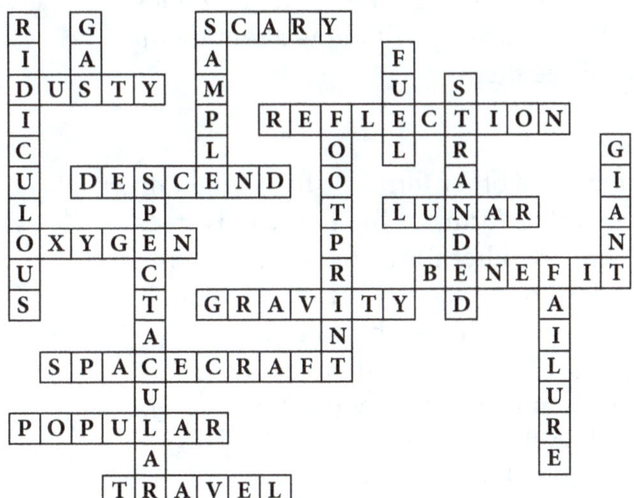

Teacher Guide

Lesson 14

ORAL QUESTIONS

Pioneer 10 went close to Saturn.

Did Pioneer 11 go close to Saturn too?

A lot of men flew into space. Are there women astronauts too?

Is it too hot on the moon for animals to live there?

Could you ever count all the stars?

Did the astronauts see any aliens?

Do you think there are other forms of life in the universe?

Did the astronauts on Apollo 13 get back to Earth safely?

Yes, Pioneer 11 went close to Saturn too.

Yes, there are women astronauts too.

Yes, it is too hot for animals to live there.

No, there are too many to count.

No, they didn't see any aliens.

Yes, I think there are other forms of life in the universe.

No, I don't think there are other forms of life in the universe.

Yes, they got back to Earth safely.

EXERCISE 1: *Some possible answers "Friend" might make.*

You: There are lots of science fiction books that have terrible aliens living on other planets. Do you think we'll find other creatures in space?

Friend: I think those are just stories. I doubt we'll find other forms of life.

You: There might be some very strange forms of life in the universe, we don't know. People could hardly believe their eyes when they saw a giraffe for the first time.

Friend: Yes, that's true, but space is not a friendly place for animals to live.

You: Yes, but we have some forms of life that live at the bottom of the ocean. They live very well under terrible conditions. They have lived there for hundreds of years.

Friend: There are terrible conditions in space. In places, the sun is burning hot, then later it is terribly cold. I don't think living things could survive those temperatures.

You: I wouldn't be sure of that! In some science fiction books there are aliens from other planets living right here, but we don't know about them.

Friend: I don't expect that I'll see them!

EXERCISE 2:

1.   Do you think that there are other forms of life in the universe?

        Yes, I think there are other forms of life in the universe.

        No, I don't think there are other forms of life in the universe.

2.   Did the Apollo missions discover any life on the moon?

        No, they didn't discover any life on the moon.

3.   Why didn't the Apollo 13 mission land on the moon?

        They had an accident that made them come home early.

4.   Did Explorer 10 land on the moon?

        No, Explorer 10 didn't land on the moon.

5. Did the scientists find out anything about how the moon was formed from the lunar landings?
    Yes they found a lot of things about how the moon was formed.
6. Is Pioneer 10 still flying away from the earth?
    Yes, it is still flying away from the earth.

EXERCISE 3:

MATCH THE MEANING

container	you carry liquids or gases in it	giraffe	an animal with long legs
long-range	stretching into the future	to explore	to travel for discovery
atmosphere	the gases around a planet	solar system	the sun and bodies orbiting it
to explode	to fly apart with a noise	terrible	very bad
expensive	it costs a lot	period	a length of time
impact	when one thing hits another	universe	everything in space

ACTIVITY 4:   PRO

They have allowed the Internet to be created.
Transportation systems depend on them for global positioning.
Communication worldwide is much faster cheaper.

CON

They are always being used to spy.
They could easily be changed to weapons.
They could easily be destroyed, and we and depend on them too much.

Lesson 15

Why did scientists need a telescope in space?

They needed a telescope that was away from the bad effects of the atmosphere.

How can scientists see the space telescope's images?

It sends the images to Earth as radio waves.

Can the Space Telescope use infra red and ultra violet photography?

Yes it can use infra red and ultra violet photography.

Are scientists able to see things that can't be seen from Earth?

Yes, they are able to see things that can't be seen from Earth.

Has the Hubble Space Telescope increased our understanding of the universe?

Yes, the Hubble Space Telescope has increased our understanding of the universe.

What is a light year?

It is the distance light travels in one year.

What was the problem when the Hubble Space Telescope first started working?

The big mirror was not made correctly.

Were the astronauts able to correct this problem? Yes, they were able to correct the problem.

EXERCISE 1:   **Fill in the blanks, using the words below**

Since the beginning of *time*, mankind has looked up and watched the *stars* .
Many years *ago* the Greeks held their first Olympic games when Venus was in a certain place in the *sky*. That was every four *years*.

When we got *powerful* rockets, scientists could *explore* the moon, space, and some of the *planets*. Now we know what the *atmosphere* is like on the planets. The *rocks* that the *astronauts* brought back from the *moon* told the *scientists* a lot about the early days of the *universe*.

From all of the space *exploration* we now know a lot more about our world.

EXERCISE 2:

1.   Where is the Hubble Space Telescope?
      It is in space.
2.   Why can the Hubble Space Telescope see things so clearly?
      It can see things very clearly because there is no atmosphere in space.
3.   How can we see things through the Hubble Space Telescope?
      We see images that the telescope sends back by radio waves.
4.   How far away is the most distant thing the Hubble Space Telescope saw?
      It is thought to be more than a billion light years away.
5.   How far is a light year?
      It is the distance that light travels in one year.
6.   What was the problem with the Hubble Space Telescope for the first three years?
      The mirror was made incorrectly.

ACTIVITY 3:

LIST 1   **MATCH THE MEANING**

1	cluster	group	13	telescope	astronomers look through them
2	great deal	a lot	14	nebula	space dust
3	light year	how far light travels in one year	15	solar system	the sun and bodies orbiting it
4	advantage	benefit	16	universe	everything in space
5	distant	far off	17	impact	when one thing hits
6	ultra violet	a kind of radiation from the sun	18	period	another a length of time
7	surprise	something unexpected	19	expensive	it costs a lot
8	gradually	a bit at a time	20	tank	you carry liquids or gases in it
9	recently	not long ago	21	to explore	to travel for discovery
10	mirror	you see yourself in it	22	long range	stretching into the
11	astronomer	a scientist who studies the stars	23	terrible	future very bad
12	to form	to make something	24	to increase	to become larger

Lesson 16

ORAL QUESTIONS

Why did they need the space shuttle?

They needed a spacecraft that could carry tools and equipment into space.

Can parts of the space shuttle be used over again?

Yes, parts of the shuttle can be used over again.

How many main parts are there to the space shuttle?

There are three main parts.

What is the cargo bay used for?

It is used to carry tools and equipment into space.

Does the orbiter fly back to Earth, to be used over again?

Yes, it flies back to Earth.

Do the solid rocket boosters come back to Earth? Yes, they come back to Earth.

Where does the crew ride?

The crew rides in the orbiter.

What color is the external fuel tank?

It is rust colored.

How many astronauts travel in the orbiter?

Usually there are five to seven crew members.

EXERCISE 1: The correct answer for each "false" answer is given.

1. The space shuttle has three parts. **True.**
2. The external fuel tank can be used again and again.
F   It can be used only once
3. The solid rocket boosters burn for nearly ten minutes.
F   They only burn for about two minutes
4. The crew rides in the solid rocket boosters.
F   *The crew rides in the orbiter.*
5. The space shuttle can carry people, equipment and tools into Earth orbit. **True.**
6. The orbiter can only be used once.
F   The orbiter can be used many times.
7. *The solid rocket boosters explode and burn up in the air.*
F   The solid rocket boosters fall to Earth, to be used again.
8. *In two minutes the shuttle is nearly 100 kilometers in the air.*
F   In two minutes it is about 45.7 kilometers in the air.
9. *The external fuel tank has a parachute for coming back to Earth.*
F   *The external fuel tank explodes and burns up as it enters the atmosphere.*
10. The orbiter burns up in the air.
F   *The orbiter returns to Earth with the crew.*
11. The shuttle can carry big loads in its cargo bay. **True.**

EXERCISE 2:
1. that could They be over over built a spacecraft used and.
   They built a spacecraft that could be used over and over.
2. in Earth The orbiter the returns to crew.
   The crew returns to Earth in the orbiter.
3. sea the solid rocket fall boosters The into.
   The solid rocket boosters fall into the sea.

4.   carrying bay tools a equipment huge There cargo for and is.
        The huge cargo bay is for carrying tools and equipment.
5.   colored is huge fuel The tank rust external.
        The huge external fuel tank is rust colored.
6.   Earth 45 shuttle minutes above the is over kilometers two In.
        In two minutes the shuttle is over 45 kilometers above Earth.
7.   on five crew usually flight to seven are members There each.
        There are usually five to seven crew members on each flight.

EXERCISE 3: *Possible* answers.

You: The two solid rocket boosters must be really powerful to lift the shuttle nearly fifty
           kilometers into the air in just two minutes. Do you think the crew is
uncomfortable? ***Friend:*** They are strapped into special seats to keep them comfortable.
You: Yes, but even with good seats, they must feel something, going up that fast! Do you think
           they get sick?
Friend: I don't think so, because they have a lot of training.
You: Yes, they have a lot of training. I guess they get used to that much acceleration. Would
           you like to go on a space shuttle
mission? ***Friend:*** Yes, I'd really like to go!
You: Yes, I'd like to go, too. It would be great to look down and see the earth below.
Friend: It would be super!

Lesson 17

How do the astronauts lift heavy equipment when they are in space?
They use the Canadarm.

How many joints does the Canadarm have?
It has six joints.

Was the Canadarm made in the United States?
No, it was made in Canada.

Was the Canadarm used to help the astronauts repair the Hubble Space Telescope?
Yes, it was.

Do the crew members sometimes ride on the Canadarm?
Yes, they often ride on the Canadarm.

Would the Canadarm be good for lifting heavy things on Earth?
No, it wouldn't be good for lifting heavy things on Earth.

The Canadarm is like a robot, isn't it?
Yes, it's like a robot.

Do the astronauts use the Canadarm to help build the International Space Station?
Yes, the Canadarm is used to help build the International Space Station.

EXERCISE 1:

1. lift engineers that tool things could a heavy The needed.
    The engineers needed a tool that could lift heavy things.
2. ride the Astronauts on Canadarm sometimes.
    Astronauts sometimes ride on the Canadarm.
3. was company by The Canadian Canadarm made a robotics.
    The Canadarm was made by a Canadian robotics company.
4. Telescope they when the Canadarm used repaired the They Hubble.
    They used the Canadarm when they repaired the Hubble Telescope.
5. excited Canadarm were the about crew new The.
    The crew were excited about the new Canadarm.
6. of Canadarm use orbiters the the All.
    All of the orbiters use the Canadarm.
7. it up night stayed to They all test.
    They stayed up all night to test it.
8. Earth controllers goodnight to said their They on.
    They said goodnight to their controllers on Earth.
9. arm was a very like strong It.
    It was like a very strong arm.
10. inside orbiter is from It the controlled.
    It is controlled from inside the orbiter.
11. equipment is heavy good for It moving.
    It is good for moving heavy equipment.
12. the in are joints Canadarm There six.
    There are six joints in the Canadarm.
13. Canadarm enjoyed crew using the The.
    The crew enjoyed using the Canadarm.
14. better expected much worked than It they.
    It worked much better than they expected.
15. is useful Canadarm a very tool The.
    The Canadarm is a very useful tool.

EXERCISE 2: CROSSWORD PUZZLE.

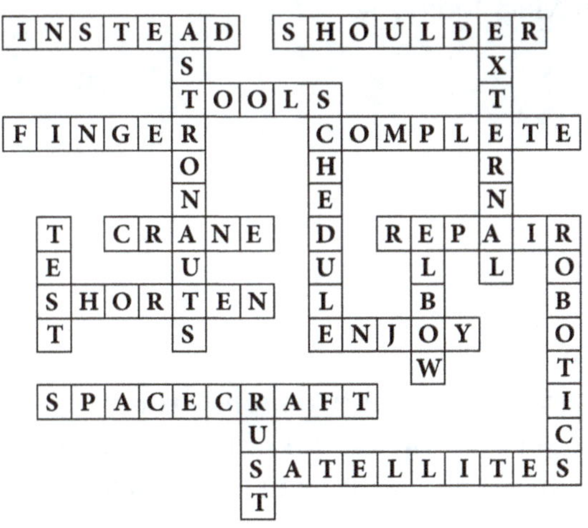

<table>
<tr><td>I</td><td>N</td><td>S</td><td>T</td><td>E</td><td>A</td><td>D</td><td></td><td>S</td><td>H</td><td>O</td><td>U</td><td>L</td><td>D</td><td>E</td><td>R</td></tr>
<tr><td></td><td></td><td>S</td><td></td><td></td><td></td><td></td><td></td><td></td><td></td><td></td><td></td><td></td><td></td><td>X</td><td></td></tr>
<tr><td></td><td></td><td>T</td><td>O</td><td>O</td><td>L</td><td>S</td><td></td><td></td><td></td><td></td><td></td><td></td><td></td><td>T</td><td></td></tr>
<tr><td>F</td><td>I</td><td>N</td><td>G</td><td>E</td><td>R</td><td></td><td></td><td>C</td><td>O</td><td>M</td><td>P</td><td>L</td><td>E</td><td>T</td><td>E</td></tr>
<tr><td></td><td></td><td>O</td><td></td><td></td><td></td><td></td><td></td><td>H</td><td></td><td></td><td></td><td></td><td></td><td>R</td><td></td></tr>
<tr><td></td><td></td><td>N</td><td></td><td></td><td></td><td></td><td></td><td>E</td><td></td><td></td><td></td><td></td><td></td><td>N</td><td></td></tr>
<tr><td>T</td><td></td><td>C</td><td>R</td><td>A</td><td>N</td><td>E</td><td></td><td>D</td><td></td><td>R</td><td>E</td><td>P</td><td>A</td><td>I</td><td>R</td></tr>
<tr><td>E</td><td></td><td>U</td><td></td><td></td><td></td><td></td><td></td><td>U</td><td></td><td>L</td><td></td><td>L</td><td></td><td>O</td><td></td></tr>
<tr><td>S</td><td>H</td><td>O</td><td>R</td><td>T</td><td>E</td><td>N</td><td></td><td>L</td><td></td><td>B</td><td></td><td></td><td></td><td>B</td><td></td></tr>
<tr><td>T</td><td></td><td>S</td><td></td><td></td><td></td><td></td><td></td><td>E</td><td>N</td><td>J</td><td>O</td><td>Y</td><td></td><td>O</td><td></td></tr>
<tr><td></td><td></td><td></td><td></td><td></td><td></td><td></td><td></td><td>W</td><td></td><td></td><td></td><td></td><td></td><td>T</td><td></td></tr>
<tr><td>S</td><td>P</td><td>A</td><td>C</td><td>E</td><td>C</td><td>R</td><td>A</td><td>F</td><td>T</td><td></td><td></td><td></td><td></td><td>I</td><td></td></tr>
<tr><td></td><td></td><td>U</td><td></td><td></td><td></td><td></td><td></td><td></td><td></td><td></td><td></td><td></td><td></td><td>C</td><td></td></tr>
<tr><td></td><td></td><td>S</td><td>A</td><td>T</td><td>E</td><td>L</td><td>L</td><td>I</td><td>T</td><td>E</td><td>S</td><td></td><td></td><td></td><td></td></tr>
<tr><td></td><td></td><td>T</td><td></td><td></td><td></td><td></td><td></td><td></td><td></td><td></td><td></td><td></td><td></td><td></td><td></td></tr>
</table>

ACTIVITY 2 STUDENT READER:

Scenario 1: Speak to this group about work safety in dangerous environments.

Scenario 2: This group might think about the implications of this in manufacturing plants, like in the car industry.

Scenario 3: Point out to this group that a lot of jobs are already done by robots. They can handle hot metals that human workers can't touch.

Scenario 4: This group could be told that the astronauts always have safety lines, so that they can't fall away from the orbiter.

28

Lesson 18

ORAL QUESTIONS

What are Spirit and Opportunity? — They are Mars rovers.

Why was it a problem landing the rovers on Mars? — They didn't want the rovers to crash.

Did the rovers take many pictures of Mars? — Yes, they took many pictures.

Is there a lot of water on Mars now? — No, there is no water on Mars now.

How long were the rovers expected to work? — They were expected to work for only 90 days. They get it from the sun.

Where do the rovers get the power to run? — They were expected to work for only 90 days. They get it from the sun.

Is it dusty on Mars? — Yes, it is very dusty there.

Was there water on Mars at one time? — Yes, there was water on Mars at one time. It takes too long to get there, and the planet is either too hot or too cold.

Why didn't they send people to Mars? — Yes, there was water on Mars at one time. It takes too long to get there, and the planet is either too hot or too cold.

Are the rovers able to find out what is in the ground on Mars? — Yes, they can dig for samples.

Do they think that there could be some form of life on Mars today? — They think that this is possible.

EXERCISE 1:

1. Why didn't the Mars rovers crash when they landed on Mars?
   They designed a special landing capsule that prevented crashing.
2. The scientists thought the Mars rovers would stop working after 90 days. Did the Mars rovers keep going after 90 days?
   Yes, they kept going for years.
3. What are the Mars rovers doing on Mars?
   They are gathering a lot of information about Mars and sending it back to Earth.
4. Did the space shuttle take the rovers to Mars?
   No, it didn't take them to Mars.
5. Why don't the rovers run out of fuel?
   They get their fuel from the sun.
6. Is Mars a dusty place?
   Yes, it's very dusty.
7. Do scientists think that there could be some forms of life on Mars today?
   Yes, they think that there could be some forms of life on Mars today.
8. Was Mars always a dry, dusty place?
   No, at one time it had water.
9. Are there ever dust storms on Mars?
   Yes, there are often dust storms on Mars.
10. Are the rovers mobile?
    Yes, the rovers are mobile.

EXERCISE 2:

Mars has an **atmosphere** that is too hostile for people so the scientists sent two **mobile robots** called rovers to travel the surface of the **planet.** These rovers send back **thousands** of pictures and a lot of **information** about Mars. They get **power** from the sun, so they won't run out of **fuel** .

29

MATCH THE MEANING

EXERCISE 3:

	it moves around	controller to	somebody who directs
	very surprising	change	something to make something
mobile	maybe	storm softly	different bad weather
amazing	what the wind does	opportunity	gently
possibly blow	to learn about something		a good chance
to study robot	a programmable machine	information	facts about something

Lesson 19

ORAL QUESTIONS

What is the International Space Station?   It is an orbiting laboratory run by many nations.
*What are the pieces of the space station called?   They are called
modules. Why does the space station have to be built*
in modules?   It is too big to be sent to space in one piece.
Do people live in the space station?   Yes, people live in the space station.
Where does the station get its electricity?   It gets it from solar panels.
Do the astronauts use the Canadarm to help
them with their work in building the space station?

Yes, they use the Canadarm to help them.

Do the solar panels always face the sun?   Yes, they turn so that they always face the sun.
Do people from different countries go and
work in the space station?

Yes, people from different countries go and
work

in the space station.

Does the space shuttle go to the space station?   Yes, the shuttle goes to the space station.
Are the scientists growing plants in
the space station?

Yes, they are growing plants there.

EXERCISE 1:

1. How do the modules of the Space Station get into space?
   They are taken there by the shuttle or by a Russian spacecraft.
2. Where does the power for the space station come from?
   It comes from the sun. / It comes from solar panels.
3. When did astronauts start living in the space station?
   They started living there in November of 2000.
4. Why is the space station made of modules?
   It is made of modules because it has to be carried into space one piece at a time.
5. Is there any gravity in the space station?
   No, there is no gravity there.
6. What do the astronauts do in the space station?
   They do research in the space station.
7. Why do the solar panels on the space station turn?
   They turn so that they will always face the sun.

8. Is there any atmosphere in space?
   No, there is no atmosphere in space.
9. Where is the space station being built?
   It is being built in space.
10. Do the astronauts use the Canadarm to help them build the space station? Yes, they use the Canadarm.

EXERCISE 2:

In the past times *mankind* always looked into the *sky*. The stars, the moon and the *planets* are so beautiful! "Wouldn't it be great if we could *fly* through the air like the *birds*!" they said. *After* thousands of flights in gliders, the Wright brothers built the *first* airplane. *Soon* people were flying *everywhere*. People then started to look at the *moon*. "We should go there *too*!" they said. So the engineers, scientists and *pilots* worked for years, and one day, a man *walked* on the moon. Today, people are *living* in space at the Space Station. Do you *think* that some day *people* will live on *other* planets?

EXERCISE 3:

1. is space panels its with station electricity that uses made solar The.
   The space station uses electricity that is made with its solar panels.
2. space new module others into of the station fits Each the.
   Each new module of the space station fits into the others.
3. the astronauts station live in space The.
   The astronauts live in the space station.
4. brought The shuttle there by the is space crew.
   The crew is brought there by the space shuttle.
5. many there are doing Scientists experiments.
   Scientists are doing many experiments there.

EXERCISE 4:

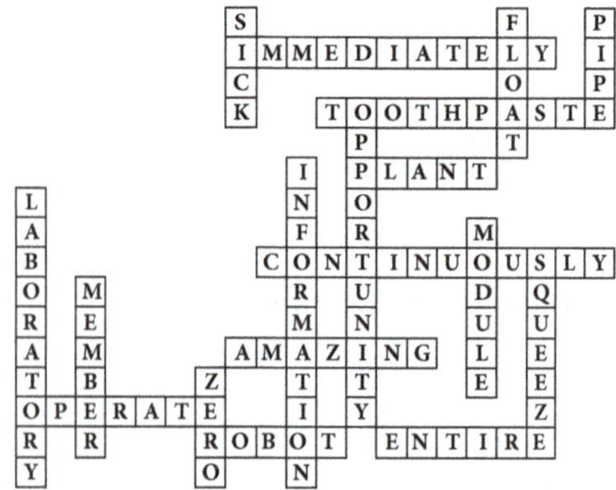

<table>
<tr><td colspan="14"></td></tr>
</table>

ACTIVITY 2 STUDENT READER:

Scenario 1: You could suggest to this group some funny effects that might be encountered in zero gravity – things like falling asleep and floating to another part of the station.

Scenario 2: Talk to this group about having their food all mixed together in a tube.

Scenario 3: This group could think of a science fiction theme in which exotic or dangerous plants grew in the space station.

Scenario 4: This group could use the space station as an example of how nations could cooperate to make Earth a better place to live.

LESSON 20 FINAL TEST

ANSWER THE QUESTIONS IN SENTENCES: (4 marks each)

1.   If you were hungry, would you go to a restaurant?
   Yes, if I were hungry, I'd go to a restaurant.
   No, if I were hungry, I wouldn't go to a restaurant.
2.   Were the early planes used for reconnaissance?
   Yes, the early planes were used for reconnaissance.
3.   If you are tired, will you go to bed early?
   Yes, if I'm tired I'll go to bed early.
   No, if I'm tired I won't go to bed early.
4.   Is airplane flight dangerous today?
   No, airplane flight isn't dangerous today.
5.   If you went to London would you visit the queen?
   Yes, if I went to London I'd visit the queen.
   No, if I went to London I wouldn't visit the queen.
6.   How could the astronauts breathe when they were on the surface of the moon?
   They had air to breathe in their space suits.
7.   A lot of men flew into space. Are there women astronauts too?
   Yes, there are women astronauts too.

Make good sentences of the words below: (4 marks each)

8.   to orbiter The work have outside astronauts the sometimes.
   The astronauts sometimes have to work outside the orbiter.
9.   are the orbiting you be hard sleep must when to earth It.
   It must be hard sleep to when you are orbiting the earth.
10.   Neil excited all the moon stepped world were Armstrong over onto when People the.
    People all over the world were excited when Neil Armstrong stepped onto the moon.
11.   there days is any in space, so no aren't There rainy atmosphere.
    There is no atmosphere in space, so there aren't any rainy days.
12.   want into go though people to is space Even it dangerous,.
    Even though it is dangerous, people want to go into space.

Fill in the blanks, using the words below: (2 marks each)

Wilbur and Orville Wright worked very (13), **hard** and they had some difficult times. People didn't (14) **believe** they could make a (15) **machine** that could fly. They made a number of small planes without (16) **engines**. These planes are called (17) **gliders**. They couldn't find an engine that was (18) **light** enough for their planes. (19)**Finally** they built their own engine. After a great deal of (20) **difficulty** they were (21) **successful**. All their hard work made them (22) **famous**.

LESSON 20 FINAL TEST CONTINUED

MATCH THE MEANING (2 marks each)

23. astronauts *they go into space*

24. disaster *something very bad*

25. cargo bay *where the shuttle carries things*

26. external *means outside*

27. crane *it lifts things*

28. tiny *very small things*

29. satellites *they orbit Earth* 31.

30. tools *you work with*

spacecraft *astronauts ride in it*

32. stranded *to be left behind* 34.

33. hill *where the ground rises*

famous *everyone knows you*

35. pilot *he/she drives the plane*

36. wind *it makes the air move*

37. history *it happened in the past*

38. to joke *to say something funny*

Visit us Online for More

https://www.efl-esl.com

BEGINNERS LESSON PLANS BOOK 1

**20 complete lesson plans
3 Textbooks plus
Downloadable Audio and
Video**

Includes:

- Student Reader
- Student Workbook
- Teachers Guide
- 20 lessons
- 5 tests
- 4 reviews
- Glossary
- Download PDF or Paperback

Book 1 Overview

BEGINNERS LESSON PLANS BOOK 2

**20 complete lesson plans
3 Textbooks plus
Downloadable Audio and
Video**

Includes:

- Student Reader
- Student Workbook
- Teachers Guide
- 20 lessons
- 5 tests
- 4 reviews
- Glossary
- Download PDF or Paperback

Book 2 Overview

Listening and Speaking Workbook

Complete Listening and Speaking English Workbook – includes full downloadable audio!

- Vocabulary for each Lesson
- Everyday Conversations – Listen to full audio then role-play!
- 14 Lessons
- 2 Review Chapters
- 2 Full Audio Tests with Answer Key
- Role Play
- Telephone Conversations and role play
- Question and Answer Dialogues

https://efl-esl.com/listening-speaking-english/

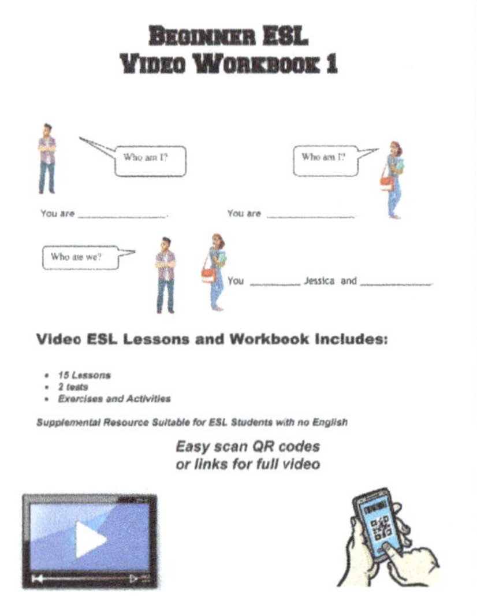

Beginners ESL Video Workbook

Includes:

- 15 lesson plans with full video
- Supplemental activities and games
- Video introduction for all topics

Learn More https://efl-esl.com/video-workbooks/

Teacher Guide

Children's ESL

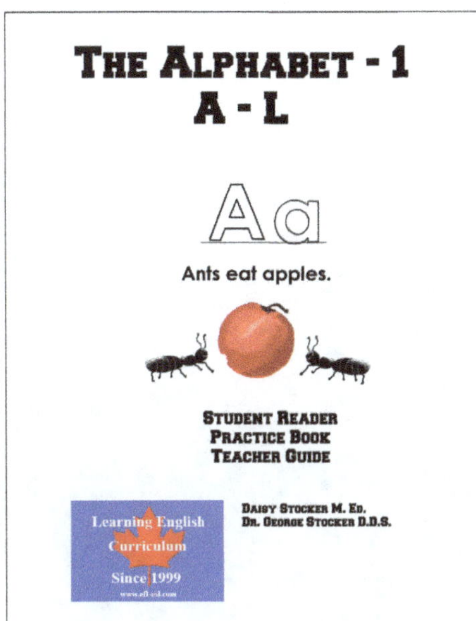

This book introduces the alphabet from A to L and the numbers from 1 – 10.

Includes:

- Student book – 37 pages
- Student Workbook – 24 pages
- Teacher's Guide Book – 50 pages
- Glossary — 142 new words
- Colorful games and activities suitable for lamination –use over and over!

https://efl-esl.com/alphabet-activities-for-esl-students/

ESL Graphic Novels for Kids (Comic Books)

These books offer an oral approach for young ESL / EFL students aged 6 - 10.

They contain high interest stories, written in the graphics novel format that children love. This is very suitable for supplementary study, home school, as well as for summer camps.

https://efl-esl.com/esl-graphic-novels-for-children/